D0433965

12382496

HEROES

100 POEMS FROM THE NEW
GENERATION OF WAR POETS

HEROES

100 POEMS FROM THE NEW
GENERATION OF WAR POETS

EDITED BY JOHN JEFFCOCK

EBURY
PRESS

*I dedicate this book to my wife Katrin
and our girls, Josephine and Franziska*

1 3 5 7 9 10 8 6 4 2

Published in 2011 by Ebury Press, an imprint of Ebury Publishing

A Random House Group Company

Copyright © in this compilation John Jeffcock 2011

John Jeffcock has asserted his right to be identified as the editor of this Work in
accordance with the Copyright, Designs and Patents Act 1988

The Random House Group Limited Reg. No. 954009

Addresses for companies within the Random House Group can be found at:
www.randomhouse.co.uk

A CIP catalogue record for this book is available from the British Library

The Random House Group Limited supports The Forest Stewardship Council
(FSC®), the leading international forest certification organisation. Our books
carrying the FSC label are printed on FSC® certified paper. FSC is the only forest
certification scheme endorsed by the leading environmental organisations,
including Greenpeace. Our paper procurement policy can be found at:
www.randomhouse.co.uk/environment

To buy books by your favourite authors and register for offers visit
www.randomhouse.co.uk

Typeset in Tibere by seagulls.net

Printed and bound in Great Britain by CPI Group, (UK), Croydon, CR0 4YY

ISBN 9780091946647

contents

SELECTION PANEL

General Richard Dannatt, Baron Dannatt, GCB CBE MC
Carol Ann Duffy CBE FRSL (Poet Laureate)
Simon Rae
Captain John Jeffcock

AUTHOR'S ACKNOWLEDGMENTS

With special thanks to: Roxanne Benson-Mackey,
Siobhan Campbell, Jasper Copping, Major David Coward,
Harry Cummins, Roger Field, Jamie Gordon,
Brigadier Mike Griffiths CBE, Michael Howie,
Christopher Joll, Major Kevin Kirkham-Brown,
Lieutenant Colonel Kathie Knell MBE, Ben Leapman,
Neil Moore, Nicky Ness, Caroline Newbury, Sean Rayment,
General Sir David Richards GCB CBE DSO,
Andrew Robathan MP, Richard Sermon MBE, Carey Smith,
Major General Sir Evelyn Webb-Carter KCVO OBE DL,
Andrew Wright.

introduction

This is not my book: it is the unheard voice of the many people who endure enormous sacrifices so that others need not suffer. They are not heroes but ordinary people in exceptional environments who risk body, mind and soul for others.

Heroes came about as I knew that others like me had written poems. I thought that a book which collated the best of these would be incredibly powerful. Seizing the moment and building on my first publication, *Book of War*, I proposed to General Sir David Richards that it would be a good idea to draw up a book of modern war poems written by injured soldiers. I asked for his support and Sir David immediately offered it. Soon the Ministry of Defence was on board.

We quickly realised that the impact of war is not limited to those who go on active service but extends to the many people, particularly families, who support them. The scope of the book was then expanded to include all those affected – a decision that has substantially improved the collection.

We have seen 250 poems from all ranks, all regiments and all three branches of the service (Army, Navy and Air Force). We received excellent submissions from regular soldiers, the Territorial Army, parents, spouses and children. Selecting the best 100 was an incredibly difficult task as every entry represented an indelible mark in the writer's life. Fortunately, we had help from Carol Ann Duffy (the Poet Laureate), Simon Rae (of *Poetry Please* on BBC Radio 4) and General Sir Richard Dannatt, each of whom ranked the poems. The scores were then collated. Difficult final decisions were made by myself.

The scores given by the professional poets and the professional soldiers varied in some places considerably. The question 'What is more important: the poetic quality or the integrity of the experience?' was brought painfully to the fore. As a soldier, I put integrity first and as a result you may find a few pieces which would not win a poetry competition but will touch you as a human being.

My view is that poetry should touch us intimately and leave the reader changed. I hope and expect the poems in this book will do that. On behalf of the writers, allow me to thank you for giving your time to hear their unforgettable new voices.

Your humble servant

Captain John Jeffcock

I

leaving

———❦❦❦———

Stay Safe

—m—

COMPANY SERGEANT MAJOR JOHN SINCLAIR (43)
Royal Regiment of Scotland, Afghanistan (Operation Herrick) 2011

I stand there looking at my child
He says to me that I am his hero
And that he loves me very much

I am rooted to the spot
I cannot move for I am close to tears
My child reaches out and holds onto my hand
As I have held his so many times over the years
And he says to me
I love you Dad
Stay safe

Acknowledgements

—◊◊◊—

CORPORAL DANNY MARTIN (28)

1 Staffords Battle Group, Iraq (Operation Telic) 2003 and 2005

My thanks to Hollywood
When you showed me John Rambo
Stitching up his arm with no anaesthetic
And giving them 'a war they won't believe'
I knew then my calling, the job for me

Thanks also to the recruitment adverts
For showing me soldiers whizzing around on skis
And for sending sergeants to our school
To tell us of the laughs, the great food, the pay
The camaraderie

I am, dear taxpayer, forever in your debt
You paid for my all-inclusive pilgrimage
One year basking in the Garden of Eden
(I haven't quite left yet)

Thanks to Mum and thanks to Dad
Fuck it,
Thanks to every parent
Flushing with pride for their brave young lads
Buying young siblings toy guns and toy tanks
Waiting at the airport
Waving their flags

Tools of War

—∿—

CROSS COMPANY SERGEANT MAJOR ALASDAIR MACDONALD (42)
Force Military Police Unit, Iraq (Operation Telic) 2002 and 2006

Bring some mettle with you, boys,
Bring packs and tools of war.
Leave love and thoughts of family be,
Your heart's no use when sore.

Bring a will of tempered steel,
For the work you face is grim.
Your brothers' fear will make you strong,
Their ends will feed the hate within.

Bring down hell upon the line,
Spit fire and fury with heart and soul.
Cast judgement in the name of freedom,
Chaos loose consumes you whole.

Bring those who fall upon your back,
Home to the arms of a nation's grief.
Lay them in their mothers' arms
And grant their loss a small relief.

Bring now strength for nights of torment,
As the battles lost and won.
Slip into dreams and rape your conscience,
Searching doubt in deeds you've done.

Bring patience for the ones you love,
For their understanding may evade.
Try again to be their memories,
Though part of you may not be saved.

Bring them hope that things will change,
That you will soon be home to stay.
That you have spent your last in foreign lands,
For a world that's lost its way.

Bring some mettle with you, boys,
You have all been called again.
Return to where your thoughts remained
And fight beside your men.

The Thousand-mile Stare

—◊—

COLONEL SIMON MARR, MBE (46)
Royal Regiment of Fusiliers,
Afghanistan (Operation Herrick) 2007 and 2010

Winding in a corkscrew of torque and pitch,
we plunged downwards from cloudless heights of blue
to roll seasick through steep banks and sharp twists.
Jagged shards of shadow and light stabbed through
our porthole views over Afghan plains.

As we landed inside the Helmand camp,
our wheels kissed the sand in metal washes of noise.
The troops rose clumsily and moved off the ramp,
swallowed from view by the sandstorm. Young boys,
wide eyes, plump faces, fresh combats, clean boots.

In this brutal patchwork of the Green Zone
it's one more unremarkable outpost.
Here, for six bloody months, far from home,
men dance with death and brush past the ghosts
who squat in the shadows of mud walls.

I twisted and squinted through the perspex pane,
but there was only dust, gravel, wire and sun.
I'd seen enough and I turned round again.
Opposite me, new shapes slumped, with their guns
laid casually over their knees.

We lifted clear to a steady hover
and then surged giddily to blue safety.
Your head feels squashed by the mounting pressure,
your ears pop and you grab straps to steady
yourself. And then we levelled and slowed.

I watched the soldier sat across from me.
His helmet was off. I studied his face.
His cheeks were hollow. Blond hair had burst free
in random clumps from his crewcut – no grace
in the fatigue lines that etched his skin.

He had a week of stubble, maybe more.
He never looked at me, but I watched his eyes.
They hardly blinked, remained on the gunner's door.
People have told me that when someone dies
you can see life ebb and then seep away.

And these eyes were losing their light, fading blue,
not even the flicker of a dying flare.
Nothing seemed to register and I knew
that I was looking at the thousand-mile stare.

War is like Tears

—◆◆◆—

RIFLEMAN NARESH KANGMANG (32)
Royal Gurkha Rifles, State of Brunei Darussalam 2011

Wiping off the brook of tears
Flowing incessantly from her eyes
I pick up my baggage with heavy heart
Heaving a loud sigh of grief
She throws her hands tightly around my waist

There is still a lot more time for dawn to begin
My son – deep in his sleep
Moths huddling around the lamp
Colliding over the same lamp
Some spreading their legs injured
While others are already dead!

Few drops of her tears
Trickle over my boot
And shimmer at the brightness of light
I close my eyes
And open them a while
To look at the boot
The teardrops flowing from my boot
Had vanished somewhere into the carpet
I think –
The life we lead as soldiers
Is like tears!

'Please do not go to the war
Let us go back to our own country'

'Don't say that, my dear!
I have promised the Union Jack – two times
How would I say
I am not going to Afghanistan?
It's my duty to go to war'
Unknowingly my arrogance slips out

I think – of my dear old parents
I see – my sleeping child
My dear wife shed into tears
Uff!
How would my heart allow me
To go to war at this time?

There is a heap of dead moths
Over the carpet
I start hearing
Soundless music
Pouring an incessant river from the eyes
And, putting a garland of flowers around my neck
With her shivering hands,
She says:
'Return from the war
Like the way you are going today'

I feel
There are many things to say
But words don't come out
Getting speechless
I step out of my quarter
And slam loudly
The door of farewell!

Back in Green

~~~

LANCE CORPORAL SEAN ROBERTS (32)
19 Light Brigade Combat Service Support Battalion,
Afghanistan (Operation Herrick) 2009

After five years away it was time to get back
Rocked up at the careers office to have a quick chat
The stripey turned round and said, 'No problem, mucker!'
Then looked away and whispered, 'Cheers, easy, you sucker!'

Within a matter of weeks I was on a plane north
With a sackful of clothes, kit, boots and so forth
Arrived in Belfast, surprise surprise, it was raining
And no duty driver to pick me up so I got the train in

I guess that really was a sign of things to come
A battalion in turmoil and coming undone
Concerns all round and a collective lack of faith
It had began to look like I'd made a terrible mistake

Out with the old and new faces galore
Perhaps the rest of the Army wouldn't laugh any more
Before the Battalion deployed on Herrick 10
Big changes happened and the boys became men

And although there's always something that makes me groan
Life isn't too bad so I try not to moan
Like on the ranges, the 'cofftea' still tastes like shit
But hey, it's warm and free, so I'll always drink it

So much has changed but then maybe nothing at all
Perhaps the changes are mine as I'm starting to get old
It's been a real challenge to get back on track
But all things considered, by heck, it's good to be back

TAle
In memory of Edward Rawson

—∿∿—

MAJOR TREVOR RAWSON (50)
Royal Electrical & Mechanical Engineers (REME),
Iraq (Operation Telic) 2009

From the self:
Yet another tiresome Tuesday working; life in monotony,
The phone keeps ringing, so many calls for me,
Out of the blue a different voice: from Glasgow APC*,
'Sir, you've been mobilised; report Monday, go to RTMC**,
We have a great job for you and it's in Iraq,
Rush away home from your desk, only five days left to pack.'

It's not at all scary, the call to arms I've waited for,
But how do I tell my wife, the Julie I adore,
How can I do this; leave her comfort for nigh a year,
It's not the thought of fighting that fills my heart with fear.

From Julie:
Travelling up to Chilwell, so very close to crying,
I will be strong, I will support; my loyalty undenying,
He is so alive, so fearless, so excited, off to do his duty,
Why should I spoil his moment, and leave feeling guilty?

From family:
Children, brothers, sisters herald me with pride,
Encourage Dad/little brother to 'go off, enjoy the ride';
'Son, it's sad you're leaving when I'm ninety-five,
Remember me for when you return, I will not be alive.'

From my boss:

'He's off next week; I dare not try stop him for sure he
    would quit,
I will have to cancel my holiday; it's leaving me in big Sh*t,
My business will lose reputation and profit; when we lose
    his skill,
We may not survive at all, my workers, my life – this will make
    me ill.'

Outbound

Waiting in Brize departure still in disbelief,
Two days of flights unfurl my view to beige desert relief,
I have a real soldiering to do, not training just for fun,
Twenty-two years of waiting; now my story's just begun.

Inbound

My work all done, I've handed off; report said 'did very well',
A part-time soldier enjoyed his tour; at last a tale to tell,
Time to leave this place; to my reality I must return,
To my Julie and the kids, my heart it starts to yearn,
Flying over England: 'What is all that green?'
'Has this really happened to me; have I really been?'
The flags soon waved; stories told but something is quite
    missing,
Yet again my dad was right, his light went out and spoilt my
    perfect ending.

---

* *Army Personnel Centre*
** *Reserves Training and Mobilisation Centre*

The Heartache of a Soldier's Goodbye

MAJOR DAVE WILSON, MBE, BEM (49)

The Rifles, Iraq (Operation Telic) 2008

The look in her eyes,
that said so much.
Tender in my arms,
and so loving to touch.

The madness of parting,
is etched upon her face.
She tries to look happy,
ever elegant, full of grace.

But I know that she's hurting,
and hiding all the pain.
So much time without her,
seems incredibly insane.

As I gaze at her beauty,
for the final time.
Six months stretch before us,
and my heart begins to whine.

She waves from the window,
as her car pulls away.
My throat starts to tighten,
a thousand things I want to say.

She mouths 'I love you,'
and in a heartbeat is gone.
My eyes almost burning,
and I know that this is wrong.

But a soldier's life
is what we follow.
Filled with danger and excitement,
but today filled with sorrow.

For I leave behind,
the love that's my wife.
My friend, my lover,
my world, my life.

The Last Letter

—◠◡◠—

SERGEANT DAVE STENHOUSE (45)

19 Light Brigade Combat Service Support Battalion,

Afghanistan (Operation Herrick) 2009

I am writing you this letter
the one that I hope you never receive
the one that I didn't want to write
the one I wanted to leave

The last letter is a letter
they recommend that you write
it's a letter for you, my loved ones,
because I never returned on the flight

But I have to tell you that I love you
and that I always will
please don't put your life on hold
on the days you just can't fill

Tell our little daughter
that I will still blow her kisses every night
and if I can ever contact her
I will try not to give her a fright

All these years of happiness
and love that we have had
you will always be my darling wife
and Megan, I will always be your dad

I'm sorry that I insisted
coming out here to Afghanistan
but I couldn't bear being left behind
and not being the soldier that I am

Yes, my life has ended
and your new life has begun
without you I'm nothing,
like an iceberg in the desert sun

When they return my coffin
please don't look inside
remember me from your memories
of when I was alive

I will cherish all my thoughts of you
and keep them close to my heart
even though I'm nothing now
our spirits will never part

I will contact you somehow
no matter what it takes
this letter is so difficult
and my heart has begun to break

I'm sorry that I left you
and we won't see each other again
the tears are flowing down my cheeks
and now the ink has run out in this pen

I Wouldn't be a Soldier

—∾∾—

Leading Seaman Radar Plotter First Class David Killelay (67)
Royal Navy, West Indies 1962 and Mediterranean 1966

I wouldn't be a soldier, fighting in a hole
I wouldn't be a soldier, acting like a mole
I wouldn't be a soldier, standing on parade
I wouldn't be a soldier, hearing that tirade
I wouldn't be a soldier, crawling in the sand
I wouldn't be a soldier, bayonet clutched in my hand
I wouldn't be a soldier, bad memories to reflect
I wouldn't be a soldier, but I'd give them my respect
I was a simple sailor; I know this may sound thick
All the time spent on the sea, it always made me sick.

Last Day of R&R

Sergeant John 'BJ' Lewis (37)
Royal Air Force, Iraq (Operation Telic) 2008

The ball's started rolling, I've turned on the tap,
I tried really hard not to as I have to go back.
The worst thing I could do was let my thoughts dwell
and consider the feelings I have for that hell.
But linger I have, let emotions come fore,
now re-check them I must, as I head back to war.
This time has been precious, a much-needed pause,
but now box up the sentiment, re-lock the doors.
Head down and stay focused, clear thinking apply,
re-cage those emotions with another goodbye.

2

active service

On Arrival in Theatre

~~~

CORPORAL DANNY MARTIN (28)
1 Staffords Battle Group, Iraq (Operation Telic) 2003 and 2005

You get to some desert place
And instantly set about trying
to capture some ugly, dangerous
insect native to there.

Once you get one
(here comes the good bit)
you find someone else who has caught their own.

With an excited, bloodthirsty
crowd gathered, you surround
them both with a ring of fossil fuel.
Then light it.

Watch them fight, man,
watch them fucking fight.

On Patrol

—∾∿∾—

COLONEL SIMON MARR, MBE (46)

Royal Regiment of Fusiliers,

Afghanistan (Operation Herrick) 2007 and 2010

How can I compel time to slow and stop
At the precise point that I step softly
Onto the carpet of treacherous sand
That has settled in this sunlit alley?

Blinking back sweat tears from darting eyes,
With a deep breath I place my boots gently
Into the remains of crumbling footsteps
Made by the men who have gone before me.

What if I could suspend all gravity
And float freely across this no-man's land?
Yet I must move like an armoured jain*
Desperate not to disturb sly sand.

But in this swollen, deafening silence
I know that I will never hear nor feel
Metal plates springing shut beneath my heels,
Triggering my moment of bloody death.

Jainism is an Indian religion that prescribes a path of non-violence towards all human beings. Its followers move slowly with the greatest of care, at a snail's pace, focused on placing their feet where they can do no harm

The Price We Pay

———

PRIVATE AIDAN MALLOCH-BROWN (25)

The Mercian Regiment (Worcesters and Foresters),

Afghanistan (Operation Herrick) 2009

Here comes the dawn, our faces are haggard and worn,
Our muscles ache, I'm not sure how much I can take,
Eyes of steel, this is so real, God bless me!!
Take away this fear I feel,
For at the first ray of light, that's when we will strike.

Just metres away the Taliban lay unaware of the terrible price
    they will pay,
Our grenades are ready, our aim is steady, my grip is tight,
    we are ready to fight,
The deafening roar, the blood and the gore,
We watch as our enemies fall, our guns blaze.

We battle on through the day; when will we pay?
The last bullet is fired, the world falls quiet, and there you lay,
    your life stripped away,
It's with great sadness we will say, we will remember the
    brothers we lost that day,
Here comes the dawn, our faces are haggard and worn.

A fire in our eyes, hearts filled with battle cries, the day is bloody
and long . . .

Finally, Babaji is won.

Rest in peace, my friend, in heaven your life will never end.

Bar One

——∿——

SERGEANT CHRISTOPHE DUCHESNE (35)

Weapons Intelligence Specialist, Afghanistan (Operation Herrick) 2010

You stare at the net above you with eyes wide but it is not the
    net you see,
Sleep will not come no matter how hard you try not to recall,
Worries fill you and fears eat at your mind,
It's there and you live it again.

A normal day doing a job with friends old and new that
    started well,
Until the world is thrown upside down and filled with sound
    and dirt,
A wall of noise picks you up and throws you to the floor in a
    fit of rage,
White dust now fills your vision and the silence is now
    deafening,
But does not last.

Cries fill the air and people shout in response but you are
    stunned,
Too shaken to move, all you see is the dirt before you,
A shake on your shoulder then a question shouted and you
    reply with a nod,
They move on and you slowly stand but the world has
    changed.

Everyone is talking bar one,
Everyone is moving bar one,
Everyone is acting bar one,
A single unit bar one.

The bag is heavy as they carry it to the waiting transport,
With downcast faces we do what must be done,
Another experience to deal with as a group and alone,
A mantra fills your head to be strong and she is waiting at home.

The alarm beside you rings and banishes the memory for now
     but never very far,
That incident is one of many and it will not be the last,
 You move with purpose and start a fresh day ready to go
     through it all again
We all do,
Bar one.

Care under Fire

—᠓—

MAJOR BARRY ALEXANDER (40)

Queen Alexandra's Royal Army Nursing Corps (QARANC) Nursing Officer,
Afghanistan (Operation Herrick) 2007

Fast jets scream in with cannon and bomb, breaking up the
enemy attack;

Blast reverberates through my entire being, rendering me deaf
and dazed

Beneath my body armour a film of mud and dust lies gritty
against my skin

An explosion rips through the compound followed by shouts of
'man down'

I have been a spectator in this gallery of hellish images, now my
work begins

I believe the first man is dead, rolling him to check brings a low
animalistic groan

With help from two of his mates, we drag him into cover

I start to check him over when I am told of another casualty

'That's four this morning.' 'How many more?'

'Are we going to get out of this alive?' 'Will I be next?'

Unanswered questions left hanging, pushed to the back of
the mind

Get on with the job at hand

The village is shrouded in smoke and fire as the company fights
    for its life
Surrounded by comrades in this maelstrom of battle I am alone
Sheltering in the lee of a compound wall as if from a mighty
    storm, ignoring the chaos
I kneel between the two living corpses and start my battle for
    their lives

Ashen faced and pallid, if I don't act fast he will bleed out
Reaching into my map pocket I pull out an emergency-care
    bandage
Sweating, shaky hands fumble and slip on the glossy plastic
    wrapper
Gripping it with my teeth I rip it open and the grey and white
    roll is free

Pressing the white pad against the groin and wrapping it tight,
    I stem the flow of blood
Binding his legs with cas straps and a jimpy sling*, all seems
    good – radial pulse present
'No morphine, boss,' he tells me. I turn to the other man, he is
    getting worse
Gasping for breath with a look of terror in his eyes

Removing his body armour shows the peppering where a
    thousand minute metal shards
have ripped through flesh and sinew, crushing lung, lacerating
    vessels
The chest seal will not stick, it slides on a body slick with sweat
    and blood, I inwardly curse the maker of a device not fit for
    purpose. Go for a chest drain, or leave it?

---

* *Casualty straps and a GPMG (General Purpose Machine Gun) Sling*

Sitting him upright brings an improvement – leave it for later –
    dress his other wounds

Unwell but not getting worse, I am winning my battle – I pause
    and observe the other

An overheated barrel brings a machine gun to a stop;
    'Who needs a piss?' the gunner asks

Three men stand over the barrel, the yellow streams sizzle on
    the hot metal and vaporise

The stench of urine mingles with hot oil and gun smoke; a sharp
    tang in the back of the throat

The gun roars back into life to cover our extraction, carrying
    stretchers out under fire

Two live casualties are strapped to the CSM's quad bike and
    taken to meet the helicopter

I have earned my pay and return to my role as spectator,
    the amateur playing soldier

Once contact is broken I trudge back to camp at the rear of
    the platoon

A film of the action replays in my head, hope I have done enough

In camp, a debrief, rifle cleaned, med kit replenished and scoff

Minimise in force – can't phone home; even if I could, what
    would I say?

Sleep comes hard, tears are shed, images of the wounded on
    my mind

A prayer for the boys on patrol tomorrow and the ones that are
    left behind

Strange Beings

—◆—

WARRANT OFFICER THEODORE KNELL (59)
Parachute Regiment

Who are these strange beings?
trained warriors,
my comrades,
my brothers,
whose special calling turns my world upside down?

for saving a life,
whether it be friend or foe, matters so much more to them
than me taking one.

A feeling of guilt rushes over me
as I watch them working frantically to save a life,
a life which minutes before I had tried so hard to take.
Torn, I will share in their sorrow if they should fail
but feel anger should they succeed,
robbing me of my kill.

Whether saving my brothers in the heat of the fight,
or wandering the killing ground when the battle is done
in search of my enemy's life to save,
their task is endless.
They spend each day covered in blood,
and every night grieving

for those they couldn't save.

These are our 'medics', half soldier half saint.

I Wanna Talk

WARRANT OFFICER THEODORE KNELL (59)

Parachute Regiment

Sitting here alone on my cot
surrounded by my friends
in a silence that is deafening
apart from the one voice that's no longer here
but now booms out around the room

Few are willing to make eye contact
but those that do quickly turn away
unwilling to share their feelings
feelings that are trapped behind their pleading eyes
eyes dancing with questions
searching for answers
answers to questions that none of us are willing to ask

We've been back over an hour now
but still we are unwilling to surrender our weapons
instead we cuddle them
like small boys with our favourite teddy
it's the only comfort we have left
providing the false safety we so desperately desire

Eventually the silence is broken,
he's the oldest and wisest amongst us
such a heavy burden for one who's still only twenty-three
'Let's get these weapons cleaned
grab some scoff
and some shut eye'

But me
I would rather sit here and talk
speak his name out loud
search for those elusive answers
shed some of this guilt,

because it coulda, woulda, shoulda been me

Combat Logistic Patrol

—◊—

SERGEANT DAVE STENHOUSE (45)
19 Light Brigade Combat Service Support Battalion,
Afghanistan (Operation Herrick) 2009

You can feel the sweat
Running down your back
As you do your five and twenties
Along the desert track

The convoy then carries on
Along the Afghanistan sands
You can count how many times
You've been out here, on both hands

Crossing the world's
Most hostile terrain
Weaving through the desert
Like a logistic train

From Camp Bastion to FOB Dwyer
FOB Delhi and Gib
Driving your vehicle
Dressed in body armour and lid

You're hoping and you're praying
That if you ever get stuck
Your mate won't be too far away
To pull you out with his truck

You've got one hand on the wheel
The other close to your gun
Driving in the heat and the dust
Blinded by the sun

Anything can happen
Within an instant

Haddock of Mass Destruction

CORPORAL DANNY MARTIN (28)

1 Staffords Battle Group, Iraq (Operation Telic) 2003 and 2005

Brain bored and arse numb
Finally the blades spun and we lifted
Skimmed the palm trees and popped flares above the Euphrates
We swooped low over the target truck
Then landed in its path

We charged in our Storm Trooper costumes
Blinding faceless shapes through dirty glass

I dragged the driver from his seat
Slammed his face into hot tarmac
Held it there with my suede boot
Steadied my hands long enough to cuff his

We searched his packed pick-up
Boxes stacked four deep five wide
Emptied in the dust on the roadside
The first box revealed ice and fish, and the next
And the next, and the last

Intelligence had said he was armed and dangerous
Armed with melting ice and defrosting cod
No match for our guns, our bombs,
Our good intentions, our morals,
Our God

We cut his cuffs, and his wife's
And left them to their ruined stock
I should demand commission
From the Taliban
For every recruit I've converted to their flock.

From a Mother

—◊—

MRS ELIZABETH BROWN (61)

Mother of two sons in the Army, one in bomb disposal,

Afghanistan (Operation Herrick) 2011

I was once your body armour
Shielded you and gave you succour.
Once protected safe within me
Now you fight alone without me
I safeguarded your well-being
Now let loose to Afghan bombing.
I wakeful try to reach afar
Connect us by a dark sky star.
Tread soft my son as you patrol
Each step that I cannot control.

Incoming!

—∿∿—

SERGEANT JOHN 'BJ' LEWIS (37)
Royal Air Force, Iraq (Operation Telic) 2008

Another familiar day turns to night,
another day closer to the homeward-bound flight.
Servicemen move around, each lost in own thoughts,
some dressed for battle, some wear nothing but shorts.

Incoming!

The siren wails with its chilling sound,
like puppets, strings cut, we all drop to the ground.
Face down in the dirt with racing pulse
we wait with the hope that the warning is false.
Alas no, too soon comes a distant thud
and with it a tremor that's felt through the mud.
More impacts rumble as we struggle to hear
if the next round to land will be anywhere near.
Throughout the attack the siren screams,
a relentless echo that will haunt my dreams.
Time stops. The ground rises with an ear-splitting crack,
senses reel, eyes tight shut, everything black.
It's OK, it was close, but this time we're safe
The rockets fell short, relief comes in a wave.
Hands shake. Alarms silence. Quietness descends.
Alone now, just waiting for the stillness to end.
The 'All Clear' is sounded, we rise from the floor
and return to the normal routine of before.

Chinese Rockets

Corporal Colin Mitchell (50)

Duke of Lancaster's Regiment, Iraq (Operation Telic) 2007

In our tent soundly sleeping
With only the noise of people breathing
Then a loud explosion
We are all awoken
It's another bloody Chinese rocket
With our base the target
The attack alarm rings out
Another night of rockets flying about
A decent night's sleep, not much chance of that
'The base is under attack, the base is under attack'
Drones the female voice from the loudspeaker
Some of the lads say they would like to meet her
I would rather not hear her tone
But be asleep dreaming of home

Life on the Floor

CORPORAL COLIN MITCHELL (50)
Duke of Lancaster's Regiment, Iraq (Operation Telic) 2007

As we talk take cover shouts someone
We hear the whistle of the incoming bomb
On the floor of our tent we lie
As the rockets and mortars land close by
One minute talking to mates
Next minute the ground shakes
Every time one lands you think shit
That was too close am I going to get hit
It's hard to describe how you feel
Nervous, worried, scared, this is no game, it's real
I've seen what these things can do
To people just like me and you
I'll never forget those times on the floor
Along with all the other things from this war
I'm just glad I can go home to my bed
Not like some of my mates who ended up dead

No Ordinary Boy

—∾—

MAJOR SUZY AYERS (53)

Queen Alexandra's Royal Army Nursing Corps (QARANC)

Head of Department for Theatres,

Afghanistan (Operation Herrick) 2006 and 2010

CAT A!*
GSW** to But-tock: no ETA
OK – I think
Where would it go, that round?
Prepare – sets, staff
Table 1 or 2 we'll see.
UPDATE!
GSW to shoulder now
ETA minutes 14 few.
OK – that's more
Chest set, Foley***
Staff be ready
Table 1 it is.
In ED we wait
Standing quiet
Ready
UPDATE!
CPR in progress;
As one we move
To my floor,
Surround table 1 – ready.
What else? He's here.
REPORT!

Then stretcher
Lines, Prep, Blade
Go In Now – where's Padre?
Heart?
Checking
Bleeding
Assessing
Stop – where's Padre?
Here, close by
With book and stole
Heads bowed all
Words of love and respect
For the one we have lost today
Goodbye sweet boy who came so far
To give his best,
He gave his all –
I never saw his face.

---

* Category A (most serious)
** Gunshot wound
*** Urinary catheter used for CAT A casualties

The Parade

—◆—

CORPORAL COLIN MITCHELL (50)
Duke of Lancaster's Regiment, Iraq (Operation Telic) 2007

Everyone is on parade again
The CO tells us we have lost another of the men
Killed in action by a bomb
We all sigh not another one
A lump comes to my throat
Quite well I knew this bloke
A picture comes to your head
You think of the last thing you both said
You feel anger, rage, then sad
And shed some tears for this lad
The padre says some words
But words don't mean much, cause it still hurts
He finishes, everyone says amen
That's one word I'll never say again

Army Life, Army Wife

—◆◆◆—

MRS LINDSEY COOPER (39)

Wife of Staff Sergeant Carl Cooper, Germany 2007–11

You love him so you follow him
That's how easy it is
Or so they think
Strange town, strange land
Only your husband to hold your hand
They don't realise you're on the brink

Posting overseas, bad news for a home bird
In private you cry so the doctor you try
You can't make yourself heard
Take these pills to ease the ache
Paint on a smile for your family's sake

When they go away it breaks your heart
You didn't marry to spend time apart
Your children pine they miss their dad
Your whole body hurts to see them so sad

You're proud of your man
He's good at this life
You try so hard
To be the best Army wife

Monthly Killed Numbers for You

—∿∿—

MICHAEL BRETT (55)

London Press Officer, Former Republic of Yugoslavia,

Bosnia-Herzegovina 1994–6

The time is blank and busy on the wall and on our wrists.

In the London Press Office, we are waiting for the news.
We are Egyptian monkeys playing with graveyard skulls.

The fax paper twitches, then slides like a seance wine glass,
Then – as if a ghost is trapped inside the drum –
Begins to whirr and clatter.

Bosnia-Herzegovina Ministry of Health.
Below monthly killed numbers for you

The letters are archaeological, dactylic,
Linear B musing beneath an arc of shells.

In their homes, 2,724. Missing 8,656.

Outside, the buses cough and grumble to Piccadilly.
An old man sweeps up autumn leaves.

More monthly killed numbers follow.

My deadline is three for the evening edition.

I take the fractured words, the question-marked numbers,
And rewrite them
In beautiful English prose
And I feel guilty, thuggish.

War Zone

—∾—

MICHAEL BRETT (55)
London Press Officer, Former Republic of Yugoslavia,
Bosnia-Herzegovina 1994–6

A grand piano lies upended, like a seashell,
On a beach of white plaster in a school hall cave
Whose roof has been torn off by the shark bite of a bomb;

And all that there ever was: shot books and magazines,
Like dead birds, lie in empty streets urged by street signs
To Keep Left and Not Drop Litter;

Traffic lights that wink like call girls at burned cars with no tyres
Smashed like glasses on bar-top tarmac,
And a tree that jumped like a ballerina in a shell-burst skirt
Dangles its roots, like knees, from the twentieth floor;

These voiceless voices, empty shoes and cables
Pulled like nerves out of giant brains, all resolve
Like a maddened symphony's second movement,
Into the purr of small arms in factory sheds and round
    street corners;

The zigzag of blood on pavements and children –
In yellow T-shirts – looking for food and parents
In the bins of abandoned hotels.

Far Away at Christmas

—◆—

CAPTAIN MARK SAYERS (71)
Durham Light Infantry and Royal Army Ordnance Corps (RAOC),
Berlin 1961–3 and Hong Kong 1963–5

Good luck you lads and lasses far away
Who bravely man the line and fight the foe.
God bless you! Have a peaceful Christmas Day!

Afghanistan: Corruption and Decay,
Heroin, Heartache . . . where life's touch and go.
Good luck you lads and lasses far away!

Lurking in shadows, those keen to betray:
Five killed by a policeman whom all know.
God bless you! Have a peaceful Christmas Day!

Grim roadside bombs which dog you on your way.
The Last Post, what our limbless undergo!
Good luck you lads and lasses far away!

Back home, the bailed-out bankers vie for pay,
MPs' expense claims: theft's new bedfellow.
God bless you! Have a peaceful Christmas Day!

Your forebears knew this bloodstained land's affray;
'Support them for we know how much you owe!'
Good luck you lads and lasses far away,
God bless you! Have a peaceful Christmas Day!

This is My War,
but No One Shoots at Me

—∿∿—

COLONEL SIMON MARR MBE (46)
Royal Regiment of Fusiliers,
Afghanistan (Operation Herrick) 2007 and 2010

This is my war, but no one shoots at me.
Weekly we meet to review strategy.
Clustered in corners of Whitehall labyrinths,
We are the comprehensive government.
Forward looking and customer facing,
We're joined up, linked in, clever and snappy.

This is my war, but no one shoots at me.
Handshakes and smiles before we take tea
(Coffee the victim of efficiencies).
Sitting in our designated places
We watch VTCs'* broadcasting faces
From the business end. They are audible,
Even visible, but still so remote.

This is my war, but no one shoots at me.
We few, we happy few, serving politely.
Sifting and shifting the words and papers
In artful mazes of prepared phrases.
All stakeholders must feel free to express
The risks, costs; departmental prejudice.

This is my war, but no one shoots at me.
We weave politics and priorities
Into strategies with ends, but no means.
Minimal resources are projected
Departmental budgets are protected.
Agreeing to disagree, we depart.

---

* *Video Telephone Conference*

CQB

RIFLEMAN DARREN MITCHELL (19)
The Rifles, Afghanistan (Operation Herrick) 2009

One, two, three, four,
Prep the grenade, kick in the door,
Five, six, seven, eight,
They try to run but it's too late,
Three, five, seven, nine,
We're in the room; your ass is mine,
Two, three, four, five,
Enemy dead, we're all alive,
One, two, three, four,
Shout to the boss the room is secure,
Seven, eight, nine, ten,
Stack up, and we're off again.

Courage

—◦◦◦—

MAJOR (42)

(*no name given, as serving in Helmand at the time of publication*)

Royal Artillery, Afghanistan (Operation Herrick) 2011

He'd seen it in the words of Owen and Brooke, the toil of war
and the lives it took,
Brave young men in far-off lands, praying to keep their legs
and hands,
Each new day heading out on patrol, exhausted courage,
strong self-control.
A constant air of toxic fear, the unseen threat ever near,
Lurking in compound or behind a boulder, a path well trodden
by Soviet soldier.

So once again out the gate, the locals quiet, some just hate,
Detesting the presence of the infidel, extreme reaction that this
soldier knows well,
Taliban, Al-Qaeda or Haqqani; he doesn't care, just wants
his family.
Just to get home to the hugs and kisses, to be with the ones that
he most misses.

Adorned like some medieval man at arms, to run the gauntlet in
the poppy farms.
Weapon loaded, ready to go, prepared to protect friend or to
kill his foe,
Then it happens, crack and blast, into cover, hard and fast,

Overhead the rounds snap and crack, the insurgents mount a
   well-laid trap,
Returning fire with due care, innocent lives are everywhere.

Then the dreadful sound of his mate's screams, that one day will
   haunt his once sweet dreams,
Young Tommy Atkins has lost a leg, 'I want my mum' he hears
   him beg,
And then he thinks of Tommy's wife and wonders if it's worth
   the price,
Is it about defending against an evil creed, or drugs or money
   or human greed,
To make this country a better place, or to defend corruption
   and avarice?

The doubt is gone, he needs to be steady, to defend his mates
   he must be ready.
And then he spies the far-off foes, a well-aimed round and
   down one goes.
Does he pray for forgiveness having taken a life? Does he hell,
   just wants to see his wife.
To survive the daily grind of battle, RPG* fire and machine-gun
   rattle.
To again emerge from this hornet's nest, limbs intact,
   no sucking chest.

And as he watches the heli depart, once again safe but sick
   at heart,
As the heli's rotors slowly thunder, this brave young man
   can't help but wonder:
Is it worth it, this human cost, young blood spilt and
   innocence lost?

So next time you see him in the street, take the time to this
young soldier greet,

Innocence, youth and friends he's lost; for one so young a
dreadful cost.

No medals or money he will expect, just what he merits,
your respect.

For he has done this for you and I, to keep us safe in this
precious isle,

And when it comes to next November, be sure to ponder and
the lost remember.

---

* *Rocket Propelled Grenade*

Decompression

—◦◦◦—

SERGEANT MARK GUMLEY (44)

Cyprus Joint Security Unit, Cyprus 2011

Poetry: what a load of shit,
Angst-ridden teen and upper-class twit.
Can't reveal my true inspiration.
Can't heal the indignation.
Who deals with the civvies' condemnation?

Primeval need to scrawl on walls.
Leather-bound books if you've got more balls.
Lust for life or butchered ear.
Pseudo-rebel, hidden inner fear.

Going postal is not your way.
Leave clock tower sniping for another day.
Can the written word purge the soul?
Light the abyss, drag from the hole?
Put some reason back into rhyme.

At least give a reach around,
when you're desecrating sacred ground.
Anal rape of the English tongue.
Can writing be construed a wrong?
Made up just for plot diversion?
Or true signs of inner perversion?
Don't reveal for honesty's sake.
The scanner has their own journey to make.

Poetry, what a load of shit?
Trenches breached, Kipling's kid hit.
Rhetorical question, no longer of this age.
Wistful wish to turn the page.

Compassionate Number

—◈—

FREIGHT CLERK CAROLINE CANDLIN (45)
Royal Logistic Corps, Iraq (Operation Telic) 2008

My dad is ill what can I do, I pack up the car as Christmas is
near, all of the presents and the rest of my gear. Don't rush
home they say on the phone, drive carefully there is still time,
but six weeks ago my dad seemed just fine.

The wind and the rain is so bad as I put my foot down and drive
like mad. Thoughts in my head of the things I should have said,
this is something in life every child must dread.

My husband's in the Falklands so far away, I need him here
to help me pray. I call that number, 'compassionate' it says,
I explain my dad is dying. They ask so many questions it makes
you feel they think you are lying.

I can't help crying as I put down the phone; they won't bring
my man home. My dad needs to die before they put him on a
plane and let him fly. As I cry I realise this is all part of being an
Army wife.

It was the 11th of December a day I will always remember.
I look at my brothers who look at my mum; I laugh and cry
as I hear everyone saying he can't be gone.

We all gather round Dad's hospital bed, all of us silent except
Mum who is screaming he can't be dead.

I ring that number once again, my heart full of sadness and great pain as I start to explain all over again. My dad has finally died can you now bring home my husband on the next flight. The guy on the phone is so helpful and reassures me my husband will be coming home, it's too late now but at least my dad won't have to be buried with me all alone.

Khukuri

—∿—

SERGEANT JAGAT NABODIT (30)

Royal Gurkha Rifles, Afghanistan (Operation Herrick) 2010

Before grooming myself
In the Army uniform
I remember – Khukuri*

Khukuri –
That has carried my story
Khukuri –
That has witnessed my past
Khukuri –
That has written my history

When I walk –
Being a Gurkha
The same Khukuri
Comes before me

Across the jungles of Burma
While we were fighting
Khukuri was the only faithful friend
Throughout the solitudes of Borneo
When we were stabbing enemies
Khukuri was the only one to defend us
In the island of Falkland
The time we ended up in a battle
Khukuri was the only reliable crutch

War:
Looking back now –
The one whacking enemies
The one saving our lives
Only was the Khukuri

A maxim goes that
After coming out of scabbard
It has to have blood.
There not only is a single incident
The history has witnessed –
Khukuri, in its best
Never dies

The whole of Khukuri has our name, and
Our name has the Khukuri on the whole.

---

* A curved Nepalese knife, similar to the machete, used as both a tool and
as a weapon

The Platoon Commander

—∾—

CAPTAIN WARREN ALLISON (29)
Yorkshire Regiment (Green Howards),
Afghanistan (Operation Herrick) 2010

He carries his weight,
He covers the ground,
He moves over shingle,
Without even a sound.

The cold of the night,
The bite of the frost,
He's reading his map,
He hopes he's not lost!

His men in position,
The ambush is set,
Dawn is fast rising,
No time for regret.

The ambush is sprung,
The rounds begin flying,
He's winning the battle,
A soldier's heard crying.

He unloads his weapon,
He's back in the base,
Safety at last,
But not joy on his face.

He slumps with his kit,
The feeling is sorrow,
One man was lost,
They're back out tomorrow.

Guerrilla Tactics

—◊◊—

MASTER SERGEANT ANTONY DALY (33)

US Air Force Reserve, Afghanistan (Operation Enduring Freedom) 2004

The enemy advances, we retreat.
Into the jungles
Into the deserts
Into our homes
The enemy camps, we harass.
Stealing their sleep
Stealing their courage
Stealing their nights
The enemy tires, we attack.
From the trees
From the sand
From the streets
The enemy retreats, we pursue.
Stealing their lives

Untitled

—◆◆—

PRIVATE ADAM STEVENSON (24)

The Mercian Regiment (Worcesters and Foresters),

Afghanistan (Operation Herrick) 2009

Kneeling here under the hot Afghan sun,
Weapon in hand and helmet on head
My back is so sore, my legs are so tired
Missing my family and missing my friends,
It seems like these days never come to an end.
Dangers around me, got to watch where I tread,
I wonder what they're doing,
If they are tucked up in bed.
I hope that they're warm and resting their heads.

I try to keep smiling and try not to frown
And when the bullets come in
I keep my head down.

I want to go home to hold my little girl again
I want to be back where my love is again.
We're nearly back in now, it's not far to go
So I pray to the Lord to let this one go
But I have a bad feeling and something's not right
So again lock and load and we resume our firefight.

Daddy's Girl

—◆◆—

SERGEANT JOHN 'BJ' LEWIS (37)
Royal Air Force, Iraq (Operation Telic) 2008

She sits there in the classroom,
hides her face behind her hair,
no one must see her eyes or note
the anxiety that lurks there.

Her father has gone away
to serve the Queen in foreign lands,
and she worries while he's gone
in ways that no one understands.

She daren't think of what he's up to,
really does not want to know,
avoiding news reports and papers
so the worry does not grow.

She keeps her feelings bottled up;
she knows that's what Dad would want,
pretend everything is normal,
show the world a valiant front.

She bravely carries on,
stays strong, she has to for her mum,
knowing she must be as worried,
missing Dad and feeling numb.

It's tough, but there's no choice,
she counts off each day as they go
until the time that he'll be back,
but the months pass painfully slow.

She's as brave as any soldier,
deserves a medal of her own,
but the only award she yearns
is to hug Dad and welcome home.

Stretcher Case

CAPTAIN JAMES JEFFREY (32)

Queen's Royal Lancers, Afghanistan (Operation Herrick) 2009

The helicopter is on the way
An example of our benevolent capability
I speak to the pilot on the radio
Briefing him on the casualty

The stretcher is laid down beneath
The father's worried old face
On it the young boy is silent
His hidden emotions leave no trace

He looks back impassively
But that cannot be so
For his bandaged right leg is
Blunted shorter, never to grow

The medics fret and fuss
Their finished work is neat
Where his foot should be now
Like a mummified head complete

He just lays there, no tears
Mouth closed, face set, awaiting
The next step of his tragedy.

First Kill

—∾—

WARRANT OFFICER THEODORE KNELL (59)

Parachute Regiment

Next in a long line of warriors
going back some two hundred years,
but this will be the first time I have felt the heat of battle on
    my face.
Moving slowly forward into contact
my one hope
my first
will be a long-distance kill.

I trust my corporal
but still my guts twist with fear.
As the distance between the two sides closes
I know that far from being fought at long distance
this
my first
will be up close and personal
fixed bayonets
hand to hand.

Nervously I select my target from those before me
I can see the weapon in his hands
the colour of his eyes
I can even hear him pant.
I pull the trigger

once
twice
and a red mist bursts from his chest
his legs give way and he begins to fall
and I brush him aside like an empty suit hanging lifeless in the air.

Like a robot I am already searching for my next target
locked on I fire again
and as I eat up the ground between us my nerves turn to fire
my blood is replaced with pure adrenalin
and as my bayonet overcomes the resistance of his shirt and skin
sinks deep into his chest
I find myself repeating,

'I am airborne,
I am my nation's best.'

Finally it ends
and in the early morning mist the killing ground falls silent.
Standing alone and drained,
combats torn by close calls and covered in blood
I survey the fruits of countless months of training.
I have my first
my second
even a third kill,
but realise nothing has really changed.

Have I made a difference in this battle?
Yes
but not the war.
I have merely robbed the world of yet another father

husband, brother, son,
and like a hammer blow to the head
the reality of my actions hits home.

Tomorrow there will be another battle
and whether I win or lose

the killing will go on.

The Ops Room Stag

—◊—

COLONEL HUGO FLETCHER (55)

16 Air Assault Brigade, Northern Ireland 1981, 82, 88–89, 92 and 95

'Oi'm ringing from Ballygawley – yer soldiers is partisan,
They're stopping all the Prodestants and niver a Catholic man,
There's terrorists, murderers, heathens, yer letting them all
    go free
But every time Oi travels, they bloody well stops me!'

'I assure you our soldiers aren't biased – it's the first complaint
    we've had,
You say we are stopping the peaceful and letting go those who
    are bad?
Our checkpoints try to be random; some are stopped, some are
    let go,'
(But unless the good all wear halos, which is which, we really
    don't know).

'If you wish to complain, put in writing your name, date of birth
    and address,
State where the incident happened – yes we'll check it with
    thoroughness,
I hope that has answered your query, we'll be in touch by and by,
Thank you for calling, good evening, yes thank you, good
    evening, goodbye.'

'He'll be "raising this in High Places", speaking to God without
   doubt,
Pass it as usual for comment – just find out what it's about,
A factual account, no emotion, just do it – don't increase
   the pain,
Oh no, I really can't bear it, there goes the damn phone again.'

'Oi'm ringing from Cappagh, Galbally, me name it is Mulligan,
Yer terrorisin' the locals, and Catholics to a man.
There's Protestants, Third Force hoodlums, all of them going
   scot free,
But always they stops Catholics, and always they stops me!'

'I assure you our soldiers are honest, we don't get many
   complaints,
You say we're leaving the wicked, and only stopping the saints.'
(My brother married a Catholic, my own best friend is a Jew,
I don't care how a man worships, can the same be said of you?)

'If you wish to complain, put in writing your name, date of birth
   and address,
State where the incident happened – yes we'll check it with
   thoroughness,
I hope that has answered your query, we'll be in touch by and by,
Thank you for calling, good evening, yes thank you, good
   evening, goodbye.'

The First Time

—◦◦◦—

CORPORAL IAN FOULKES (47)

Royal Corps of Signals, Northern Ireland 1998–2001

Hands, fumbling with zips and buttons. An ecstasy of fumbling. A sense of urgency, wanting, almost desperately needing to get it done, to be rid of these cumbersome clothes. Then the wait and the anticipation giving way to anxiety, exertion. Worrying if I will be good enough. Concerned I will fail at the last minute. Then a half hour later . . .

I look around the small room, clothes strewn about it haphazardly.
Picking up the vest I had discarded on the floor just a short time ago and folding it neatly away.

The sweat of recent exertion, my heart still pounding. Still trying to catch my breath, after all the excitement.
A thought, I am not the first and I certainly won't be the last.

Hands still fumbling with zips and buttons. Zips and buttons I have handled God knows how many times for God knows how long without a problem.
Now they are mysterious and confusing. They refuse to obey my simple commands. That's why my hands are shaking like a drunk with the DTs.

A half hour before, a hard-as-nails feeling, now just washed out and used up. Tension gone.

A soft voice: 'Ian, are you OK?'

'Yeah I'm fine,' I reply. 'You?'

'You know how it is.'

'I do now.'

Still seeing those green eyes, her face one of the most beautiful I have ever seen. A lovely voice saying ugly things. Then she threw in my face her used sanitary towel.

'OK, Corporal F, ten minutes and get the lads in for debriefing.'
A pause, then he adds, 'Crossmaglen is always a bit of a bastard the first time . . . you did well.'

Yes, it is a bastard.

Incident Report – Road Patrol, County Fermanagh

—∿∿—

LIEUTENANT COLONEL ROGER AYERS, OBE (78)

Royal Artillery, Northern Ireland 1977–9

We stopped, and getting clear
    Of vehicle and headphone noise
I stood and listened to a bird that sang.
    The notes rang
Quelled, and then dispelled
    Clouds in my mind.

The sky, too, cleared and the bird sang on, while
    The ground, green dressed,
With recent rain caressed,
    Warmed in the sun's slow smile.
So I, and my taxed
    Body and mind
                        Relaxed.

But yet, while my bird sings,
    The ops room telephone rings.
The radio chatters, and shatters,
    In manner rude, my mood.

The ready engines roar
    Before I've slammed the door
And only the active eye, alert to map
    And chance of hedgerow trap,
Betrays the inner fear
    I struggle not to hear.

We are first at the bomb's burst
    And when we prove it clear
I draw near, and peer, and see
    In shattered vehicle shell,
Fresh
        Dead flesh.

In the face of death, I draw breath
    And smell – Ireland, and Hell.

Hate

—◆◆—

WARRANT OFFICER THEODORE KNELL (59)
Parachute Regiment

A tiny border town awakens from a less than peaceful night.
The sangar on the police station roof gets a new tenant
one who minutes before
had been dragged wearily from the clutches of a giant green
    maggot
to spend the next two hours
sweeping the countryside across a rifle sight.

A mixed Army–police patrol moves quietly through the town
while locals go about their business.
A young woman
not much more than a girl
danders in front of me with a child.
I watch them laughing
and for the briefest moment I forget where I am,
the flack jacket and the gun in my hand.

A screech of tyres forces me back to reality
turning around
just in time to see the rear window of a car being slowly wound
    down.
Automatic gunfire shatters the fragile peace.
Grabbing the young mother and her child on the run
I bundle them into a shop,
and as I fall on top of them

I am showered in broken glass and stone chippings
as bullets smash through windows,
and crash into the brickwork of the tiny shop.

But before we can respond
return fire
they are gone
back into the South
and it's over.

I help the mother and her uninjured child up off the floor
but am totally unprepared for her reaction;
as she heads quickly towards the door
with hatred burning fiercely in her eyes,
she spits in my face and shouts loudly

'Take your hands off me, you British bastard'

then pushing me aside
she leaves the shop
uninjured
with her precious child.

I remember thinking,
'Just how much do these people hate us?'

Belfast School at 3 a.m.

CAPTAIN RODDY CAMPBELL (47)
Royal Artillery, Northern Ireland 1990

Cold night rain drips
On the tin roof.
Some comes through and puddles at our feet:
Each drop a thud
Louder than our stealthy footfalls
In the smoking school.
And the orange streetlamps shining through the windows
And the winter rain outside.

Where's the fire?
What is it?
A smouldering wastebin?
A prank?
A frayed wire?
Or – the dread that fills us all
And chokes each minute
In sixty long-drawn seconds –
Is it It?
A 'come-on'?

I saw him just last Tuesday.
Brave-as-you-like.
He Came On, just like now.
They got him out.
Sirens screaming, passers-by

White-faced passed his stretcher.
I saw his head.
Could have been anybody's but I knew it was him.
Because he's blond.

Is this It, Now?
The rain drips.
Am I the next Him?
The seconds tick.
Each of us straining,
Listening in the orange gloom
Smelling the smoke,
Waiting for the white flash
And hearing nothing but the rain.

The Journey

—◦—

SERGEANT DAVE STENHOUSE (45)

19 Light Brigade Combat Service Support Battalion,

Afghanistan (Operation Herrick) 2009

Let me take you on a journey
away from your home
away from TV
your family, your phone

Follow my words from this poem
in which I write
keep your eyes open, and let me take you to Afghanistan at night.

The young soldier you see
has been cut down in his prime
hit by an explosion
he hasn't got much time

That's his best friend beside him
holding back his tears
it was only last month they were out
having a few beers

The medic is trying his best
to stop the fast-flowing blood
as it gushes from his ripped-apart body
into the sand turning it to mud

He's crying for his mother,
daughter and wife
far away from his family
only moments left of his young life

The medic still tries his utmost
but the young lad is dead
his best friend beside him
releases his grip, and bows his head

You must return home now
as your family is all alone
perhaps you will see this young soldier's family
waiting by the phone

The Interpreter

—∿∿—

COLONEL SIMON MARR, MBE (46)
Royal Regiment of Fusiliers,
Afghanistan (Operation Herrick) 2007 and 2010

We are driving from the airport to the city;

No sir, my family are not with me,
he says. They live in London – Twickenham.
It has been our home for more than ten years,
a few minutes' walk from the stadium.

He stares keenly out of the window as he talks;

My home village can be found in Kunduz,
he says. That is to the north of Kabul.
Kunduz has always been a rich province.
It is well developed with kind people.

He has answered these questions many times before;

My parents, insha'Allah, are still alive,
he says. Sometimes I go and visit them,
but I am very busy with my work.
There is also some trouble in Kunduz.

His elegant fingers hold onto his seatbelt;

My family are healthy, thank you, sir,
he says. My children attend the local school.
They speak like the English and are happy.
No, they have not visited Kunduz.

The chinstrap on his helmet bounces off his throat;

It is not such a bad way to live, sir,
he says. I can earn money with this job.
Three years I have been working as a 'terp';
sometimes I can go home for holiday.

We watch a convoy of army pick-ups speed past;

No one can say what will happen here, sir,
he says. These people just want peaceful lives.
But there is trouble, always some trouble.
They hope, but they do not know who to trust.

Our patrol is waved through a new police checkpoint.

In a Different Room

CORPORAL JOHN LEWIS

Iraq (Operation Telic)

I see the same stars,
I see the same moon,
As it just happens,
I'm in a different room.

The sun still shines,
The birds still tweet,
It's the same old ground,
Beneath our feet.

My heart'll never dwindle,
My love'll never fade,
Home is where the heart is,
Regardless of where I'm laid.

I can see your faces,
I can feel your smiles,
I'm always near you,
Give or take a few miles.

I think the same thoughts,
I feel the same gloom,
I'm always with you,
I'm just in a different room.

Tree Sonnet

—◊—

COLONEL HUGO FLETCHER (55)

16 Air Assault Brigade, Northern Ireland 1981, 82, 88–89, 92 and 95

If you have been to Shorabak, you've seen
The Afghan soldiers there have planted trees.
The nomad loves the genie of the green
Who plays when bushes shiver in the breeze.
At Bastion we eat the purple dust,
Trees are forbidden pleasures. We are not fussed
How barren is the earth, how hard the toil;
We are not here to plough the Afghan soil.
To plant a flower is not why we came,
To love a garden, or to sit in shadows.
We seek the exit door that ends the game,
Not Xanadu or fertile upland meadows.
But could I only hear a songbird sing
On some green bough, my heart would soar, take wing.

Invisible Soldier

—•—

CORPORAL VINCENT POLUS (32)
Royal Regiment of Scotland (Black Watch), Iraq (Operation Telic) 2003, 2004
and Afghanistan (Operation Herrick) 2009

The sniper roams the battlefield
A modern-day warrior assassin
His sword a high-powered rifle
He'll make his enemies yield

An armoured vehicle his chariot
His own two feet his steed
He melts into the background
To hunt his prey, his need

From his final fire position, invisible to enemy eyes
Gazing across the smoke-filled land, he sees, first two,
   then four, then five
Unsheathe my sword, bring the hammer back
Control my breath, feel my chest rise

Looking down my X12 sight I predict each step he takes
I release my sword and wield it straight and true
The hammer drops, pin strikes round, oh what a sweet sound
   it makes
One second passes, nearly two
I watch him fall from a mortal wound through the dust and
   smoke and hue

His four comrades confused and afraid fare no better
They run left and right but all four falter
I see the sheen from their brow from sweat, wetter and wetter
I'm determined to win, I don't wane, and my course won't alter

The five men are still and in everlasting sleep
They are with their god who will be their judge
My job for now is done, my task complete
Will there come a day for me to weep?
When it's my turn and I'm at the gates in front of St Peter
I'll put my heels together, hold my head high and pray I've done
    enough to avoid the heater

Cat or Mouse?

——~~——

WARRANT OFFICER THEODORE KNELL (59)

Parachute Regiment

Hello
I see you across the canal

I see you over the fields
their sparse grass blowing gently in the wind

I see you
sitting amongst the ruins of the compound
its crumbling walls providing little respite against the heat of a
midday sun

I see you
crouched low behind a pile of mud bricks
your rag-covered head
your cheek resting on the Dragonoff
your eye glued to its sight
while you try to see me

But you don't see me
lying in this hole
half covered by stinking mud
quietly watching the dust swirl across the track
judging the wind
the range
continually adjusting

I take a breath
exhale
hold it
and squeeze

another place
another time
maybe you and me be mates

Goodbye

They Pumped the Chest of the Dying Soldier

MAJOR DAVE WILSON, MBE, BEM (49)
The Rifles, Iraq (Operation Telic) 2008

And they pumped and they pumped,
And they pumped in vain.
As the soldier on his back,
Lay still in the rain.

On a cold wintry evening, as the rain lashed and more,
The darkness engulfed us, chilled our bones to the core.

An incident had happened, the radios informed.
So we raced to the area, a soldier to be mourned.

And they pumped and they pumped,
And they pumped in vain.
As the soldier on his back,
Lay still in the rain.

The scene was dark and gloomy, apart from lights flashing blue.
One glance told a story, this young man's life was through.

He was lying still upon the ground, chest bare and pasty white.
The rain bounced all round him, as his soul ebbed out of sight.

And they pumped and they pumped,
And they pumped in vain.
As the soldier on his back,
Lay still in the rain.

The life was draining from him, before they cut him free,
The fight to save him pointless, plain and clear for all to see.

So they pumped at his chest, as he lay in the rain,
Cold and still, never moving again.

And they pumped and they pumped,
And they pumped in vain.
As the soldier on his back,
Lay still in the rain.

Last Dawn in Afghanistan

———

PRIVATE KEN PICKLES (72)
Gordon Highlanders, Cold War

To Helmand I came as part of a game
With high stakes for the long-term duration;
Straight limbed, just nineteen, smart, incredibly keen,
And I manned the ob post off the station!

The attack came at dawn when the sky was first flush
And the trees and the enemy moved lightly,
But we fought them like hell, drove them back for a spell,
Then rested and closed our ranks tightly.

When a suicide bomb blew me flat on my back
I thought upon Christ's second coming;
So I called for my mum thinking surely she'd come
As the chopper propellers were humming.

Once inside I felt calm and this nurse held my arm.
Speaking softly like an angel in heaven;
Her scent was divine – of flowers and pine
And I held to her breast like I was seven.

As we sped through the air I hadn't a care.
Holding tightly her hand, feeling colder,
But she didn't mind for she knew I was blind
And I died in her arms like a soldier!

Realities of Army Life

—∿∿—

HAYLEY HARRISON (25)

Wife of Captain Adam Harrison, Iraq (Operation Telic) 2008
and Afghanistan (Operation Herrick) 2011

The lonely bed beside me
as the days, the weeks fade away.
Knowing you will return again,
but how long will you stay?

The loneliness inside me,
my heart has lost a piece.
Why steal you away from me?
'For the sake of war or peace!'

The minutes turn into hours
as I lie awake in the dark.
Stroking the empty loneliness
where you once used to leave your mark.

The Army may be your career
But I am your wife.
To have, to hold, I stood before you
and pledged the rest of my life.

So I'll wipe away the tears
as they roll down from my eyes.
As from the moment you fill the emptiness
I will feel complete once more!

An Unwanted Gift

WARRANT OFFICER THEODORE KNELL (59)

Parachute Regiment

His little body shakes in anticipation
so eager to please
running along the narrow streets
searching every crevice
hoping to find his prize.
Personally I hope he doesn't

He's got something
'Good boy',
you think so?
Now it's my turn
but I'm not so eager.
Let's hope it's on its own,
but knowing my luck,
it'll be what some sick bastard named a daisy chain

Buried at the foot of a wall
perfectly placed to channel the blast along the narrow street,
catching as many as they can,
but they're too late
the boys have gone to ground
well back,
and like meerkats,
with eyes wide
and heads on a swivel,

they now scour the area
protecting me like some precious jewel

Laying here alone
with my sweat soaking into the sand
I empty my mind of everything,
even my wife and son
everything, except for the job in hand.
Gently I clear away the earth
picking at it, like a child with a meal it doesn't want,
slowly exposing the deadly gift that's been left for us
lifting each wire in turn
looking for those tell-tale signs
the ones that will tell me it's not alone

Please God, keep my hands steady

I've only got a week to go

Sir

In memory of Lieutenant Colonel G.R. Elsmie

—∿—

CORPORAL ALEXANDER PARK (71)

Gordon Highlanders, Second World War (Japan) 1942

Sir, I cannot feel my legs
Hush son and save your strength
the CO frowns and begs
Sir, I cannot move my arms
Hush son and save your strength
the CO whispers with his charm
Sir, I cannot see the sky
Hush son and save your strength
the CO wept, then you will not see me die
Sir, I cannot hear you, sir
Sir, I cannot hear you, sir

The Mask

—◆◆◆—

SERGEANT JOHN 'BJ' LEWIS (37)
Royal Air Force, Iraq (Operation Telic) 2008

Get a grip! I'm expected to succeed,
face fear, be strong, and take the lead,
not hesitate in thought or deed.
My mask must never slip.

Man up! and keep my thoughts inside
No one can know how much I cried
when the rockets came and the fear arrived.
My mask must never slip.

Crack on! There's no time to reflect
or admit that I did genuflect
and prayed to God, me to protect.
My mask must never slip.

Chin up! Worry not 'bout how I feel
Never let them know just how surreal
it was. Dark thoughts I can't reveal.
My mask must never slip.

Special Delivery

—∿—

WARRANT OFFICER THEODORE KNELL (59)
Parachute Regiment

Surrounded by my friends
but still I am alone.
The chatter and laughter that once was commonplace
has dissipated
to be replaced with an absolute silence
broken only by the clatter of the old Dakota's engines.

Looking down on the world as it silently rushes by
I can do little but wonder at its raw beauty,
then feel sorrow
at the pain and suffering far below,
and the thought of what may be to come.

Maybe they won't need us today?
I live in hope.
But if they do,
it is I who must take that first step into hell
and pray that I reach the ground
before the fatal round finds me
whilst I hang helpless in the air.

I comfort myself
by thanking God that I only have to jump
and not fight my way off a landing craft
through water thick with blood and bodies
in a desperate bid to reach the false safety of some foreign beach.

Prepare for action; stand in the door; red on;

bugger, it's turned to a bag of shit
and now it's my turn
to jump and do my bit

Green on; GO

Some Help Here, Please!

—∾—

WARRANT OFFICER THEODORE KNELL (59)

Parachute Regiment

Hello God it's me again.
I know I only call when I'm really in the shit
but at least you know you're needed
and I'm not faking it.
I've heard men call your name
when they're about to jump;
they promise to never drink again,
to go to church every Sunday

if you'll only let them survive the fall
and live to see just one more day.

But with me you know it's different
I only call when it's something really big,

well God today is one of those days.

I know you're busy elsewhere
with other
more deserving lives to save
but you must have heard that bloody great bang
and seen the white plumes of our phos grenades

To say we're outnumbered would be a bit of a joke
the firefight's in full swing now
the air full of buzzing bullets
and thick with acrid smoke

I have two dead
and of the four that are left
two of us are carrying fresh wounds
so as you can see
we're in well over our heads

I've spoken to Zero
he says they're on their way
but it could be some time
so it would be really good to get a second opinion
as to whether I'll live to fight another day

anyway God,
needs must
things to do and lives to take

thanks very much for listening
but I suspect the next time we talk

it could well be
face to face

The Ensign and The Plank

—◆◆◆—

PETTY OFFICER STANLEY KIRBY, BEM (DIED IN 2009)
Royal Navy, Second World War (poem written in 1947)

You've pulled a man from the freezing sea all black with
    ship's oil fuel
You've cleaned him off, and see his wounds and wondered
    what to do,
You see the whiteness of his ribs where steam has skinned
    him too.
The guilt you feel when you look at him feeling glad it isn't you
And all you have to ease his pain is aspirin and 'goo'.

You fear to look him in the eye for the question you know
    will be there
The answer you know is certain death, and there's nothing more
    you can do.
You light him a fag, and give him your tot as he looks for the rest
    of his crew.
Then you lay him out on the iron deck knowing that's his lot
Briefly wondering if you did aright by giving him your tot.

For the rest of the watch, with a sail-maker's palm, with needle
    and with thread,
You sew him up in canvas with the rest of that night's dead.
With a dummy shell between their feet, making certain that
    they will sink
You sit and sew till the morning's glow, amid the mess and stink.
By dawn's grey light you carry them aft, to the ensign and the
    plank.
And the hands off watch gather round all bleary-eyed and dank.

Then the skipper with his Bible says a sailor's prayer
Our Father which art in heaven (we hope you're really there).
One by one the dead are gone, slid from the greasy plank,
A second's pause and then a splash, they sink beneath the main.

The hands go forward, feeling chill, thinking of those that
    were slain
with a certain knowledge in a while we'll do it all again.
Each one being still alive, breathes a silent prayer of thanks
Wondering, with a cold dark fear, will I be next on the plank?

1944

~

ABLE SEAMAN RALPH WOOLNOUGH (86)
Royal Navy, Second World War 1944

Orcadian ships dissolve in the mist,
Sea boots and duffels the rig of the day,
As sheep ridden, fleet hidden
Sleety old Scapa falls quickly away.

We abseiled the west coast
Turned left at Land's End,
To a warm Channel berth
And a quiet make and mend.

Dropping the hook
And a few old neuroses
Near neat Hampshire gardens
Alight with May roses.

To come were the prayers
Of the padre at night,
And a buggered-up beach
In the June morning light.

And the skipper's speech
About beaching the boat
To still use the guns
If the sod wouldn't float.

And unwashed days, and fucked-up nights,
And bodies drifting down the side
On a green sea and slow swell
Of sad detritus on the tide.

As the years turn
And I reach November,
It's still the roses
I remember.

Padre

—◆◆◆—

ABLE SEAMAN RALPH WOOLNOUGH (86)
Royal Navy, Second World War 1944

Praying for their safe return
Made me feel better
And perhaps cheered them too.
    Not all of course,
Just a shit-scared few
Of the faceless lumps
Hunched down in the dark.

Sheep
Heading for the shambles.
Fagless, seasick, shoulders stiff
From the salt-wet webbing
Binding the weights
That would drag them down.
    Not all of course,
Just a few would drown.

I wasn't good at names
But still remember some.
Chalky, Nobby, Chock . . .
And Yorky
Who died still calling for his mum.

I never really fitted in:
Never had the touch.
High-churching with the Dean for years
Hadn't taught me much.

They wanted what I couldn't give,
A cheery, hearty sort of bloke
Who'd earn respect
But still could share a dirty joke.

    I did the best I could.

They died untidily,
But now they lie in ordered rows
Of regimental symmetry.

I come back still
To pray for them
    And hear their distant laughter fade
    When I approach

    Just as I always did.

The Price We Pay

—◆—

LANCE CORPORAL GARETH JAMES (23)
The Mercian Regiment (Worcesters and Foresters),
Afghanistan (Operation Herrick) 2009

As the darkness breaks into dawn
Faces appear tired and worn
Of men that were once young and innocent
But eyes now tell a whole new story
Things they've seen and done
Still not totally absorbed

Some look around and ask
Where friends are now
Not ready to accept they have gone
But maybe they are the lucky ones
To now be free of this tragic world
Where freedom comes at a high price
That seems only to be paid
By the good and the brave

'Only the good die young'
Is what they say
But how good must you be I ask to die so young
As young as Robby and Gav
As good and brave as Sandy
But I guess these are the ones who are truly free
Long gone but never forgotten

The rest of us remain here holding the line
And still paying the price
For everyone's freedom
But our own

Loss

—◆—

WARRANT OFFICER THEODORE KNELL (59)

Parachute Regiment

Like tired ghosts we appear
one by one from the darkness of night.
The moon slides behind a cloud hiding our arrival
while the trees carry our grief
helped by the earth
which now cradles the empty shell that once was my friend.

Quietly we cry
not like children who've lost a favourite toy
but as men
here to bury a brother
a warrior
and my best friend
who in the eyes of his mother
will always be just a boy.

Your courage
humour and compassion
even in the face of great adversity
is the stuff of regimental legends.
That infectious laughter
like your generosity and love
along with my guilt of having survived
will walk with me always.

The service must be short my friend
much shorter than you deserve
for we still have things to do.
As you lie here alone in this simple grave
with the frost gnawing on your bones
just remember
I promised I'd not forget you
I will return and take you home.

When all has been said and done
those of us who remain will disappear
like the morning mist at the dawn of a summer's day
to spend it laid up
in hiding
waiting
until once more the darkness becomes our friend.

When I'm asked
why do you grieve so?

my mind will return here
to your freshly dug grave

and I'll answer quietly

because with the loss of every friend my world grows a little
    dimmer

and I've spent far too long in the dark already

The Reserve Platoon

SECOND LIEUTENANT JOHN WARBURTON

The Rifles, Afghanistan (Operation Herrick) 2010

The reserve platoon whistles a different tune,
Found at the back, lying in wait
Waiting to be called, to move fast, shoot straight.

In echelon assault, we will not fault,
Save the best until last,
Patience, not revolt.

A coiled spring, biding its time.
Saving the company,
It's our time to shine.

3
coming home

In Memoriam

—∽—

MAJOR BARRY ALEXANDER (40)

QARANC Nursing Officer, Afghanistan (Operation Herrick) 2007

News of your death came in fragments
The news told me a 'Viking' had fallen
I heard on the grapevine it was C Company
At KAF* I found out it was you

I shall never forget you, who made a stranger welcome
Unflappable in the ops room, managing chaos
Shirt off, cigarette lit, sporting a boyish grin
Combat took you before smoking could

I should have been there
Could have tried to save you
Would it have made a difference?
Would being there have changed anything?

I saw your repatriation
Met your parents
Laid Minden Roses at your grave
Is it not enough?

Does time really heal?
Four years have passed
Memory of you has not
Eternally young and courageous

You earned your peace
Have I?

---

* *Kandahar Air Field*

Unmentioned in Dispatches

—∿∿—

MASTER SIGNALLER IAN FISHER (67)
Royal Air Force, Gulf War (Iraq) 1991

Some of them never come home to fanfares,
they dump their kitbags down at the door,
kiss their wives and let their children
wrestle them down to the kitchen floor,
switch the telly on, pour out a whiskey,
search for the local football score.

Some of them skip the quayside welcome,
dodge the bunting and cannonade,
make their landfall in silent harbours,
nod to the coastguard, but evade
the searchlight of public scrutiny
like those engaged in the smuggling trade.

Some of them land at lonely airfields
far removed from the celebration,
hang their flying gear in a locker,
cadge a lift to the railway station,
make for home and take for granted
the short-lived thanks of a grateful nation.

Some of them miss the royal salute,
the victory parade along the Mall,
the fly-past, the ships in formation passing
the cheering crowds on the harbour wall.
Remembered only by friends and relatives,
some of them never come home at all.

My Girl is Waiting

—◆—

MEDICAL ASSISTANT MICHAEL BEAVIS (26)
Royal Navy (serving with Royal Marines), Afghanistan (Operation Herrick)
2007 and Iraq (Operation Telic) 2008

And so finally we're pulling into the station.
My heart is pounding
My girl is waiting

Six months ago I left her standing where she stands now,
Trying to find strength,
To let go somehow

And with tears in her eyes and a voice of despair,
Another broken heart, now beyond repair

How she has waited for me I will never know,
Just keeping it inside
Letting only courage show

And now all that separates us is the carriage I'm in,
The noise of returning soldiers, a comforting din

And with a hiss, the train doors finally do part,
We make eye contact
A skipped beat in my heart

As I reach for her, and she says my name,
Six months of pain are washed away, like a gentle summer's rain

I hold her now and time stands still
An empty vessel, my heart
Only she can fill

And with a hiss of engines the train gets underway, moving
   down the track the carriages sway

As I look back I see another soldier
He smiles with his wife, so close he now holds her

And in the back of my mind I know the day will come,
When I have to return to the sand and the scorching sun,
For this is the course we have chosen to run
But now with this war, my duty is done

Duty now lies only with her,
My love, my protection
And back in my care

I can never tell her of the horrors I have seen,
She could never comprehend
How I have longed for her. So broken.
Wounds only she can mend

She doesn't ask questions,
No truth she seeks
Her hand through my hair and a kiss on my cheek

And tonight in each other's arms we lay,
I thank God I can hold her

What Would You Know?

―∾―

CORPORAL DAVID WARRILLOW (40)

The Rifles, Afghanistan (Operation Herrick) 2009

You go to work,
You go home,
What do I do?
I'll tell you, shall I?
I work, we work,
I have Mr Death stood by my side,
Waiting ever patiently for the one mistake.
Who am I?
You know me,
You've met me,
You've maybe just seen me,
In the street,
In a shop,
In a pub,
On the front of your newspaper,
That one you read every morning,
You turn the page,
All that's mentioned is the dead soldier's name,
All he gets is ten lines on page six!
Footballers get the front page and the next five for sleeping with
    a whore?
There's no mention of the six injured the day before,
An IED, a shoot, an RPG.
What's an IED? I hear you ask.
I'll tell you, shall I?

It's a bloody big bomb!
One mistake away from Mr Death.
Do you really give a damn?
No, of course you don't.
It's my neck on the line, after all, not yours!
Remember bullying me at school?
Didn't think you would.
When you see me, it's scum you see.
Who's the scum, you or me?
You say me,
Well I say you!
You see us in a pub,
God, they're too loud
God, they're too rowdy,
YOU SAY!!
See him there?
Yes him,
The lad in the white shirt?
He was holding his mate's head together two weeks ago.
His mate,
My mate,
Could've even been your mate!
Died in his arms,
Died on his lap.
He died to protect your country,
He died to protect your livelihood!
What would you really know?
What would I know?
More than you could possibly ever comprehend!
You have no idea,
What would you actually know of the real world?
Absolutely NOTHING!

Eight Thousand Miles Away

—〜〜—

CAPTAIN ROGER FIELD (55)

Blues and Royals, Falklands War (Falkland Islands) 1982

'You're my hero,' she said.
Surprised me. Threw me. Flattered me.
But I'm no hero. I survived. Did all right.
The heroes are dug into the peat eight thousand miles away.

'You are. You're my hero,' she said.
What to say? How to give her what she wanted?
What I wanted,
After months spent eight thousand miles away.

'Was it cold?'
'Of course it was fucking cold,' I wanted to say.
But could not.
Not here. Not now. Pretty girl. Silly girl.
My thoughts now eight thousand miles away.

All so easy. Smile and play the fool?
Get what I wanted?
What I so badly needed.
But could not betray what I left eight thousand miles away.

A Hero Returns

—∾∾—

MAJOR SONYA SUMMERSGILL (43)
19 Light Brigade Combat Service Support Battalion,
Afghanistan (Operation Herrick) 2009

His kitbag is packed, he's coming home,
No more this futile land shall he roam.
Laughter fills the plane, which he sits on,
His first sight of England is at Brize Norton.
He studies the waiting throng for a face,
The panic within him makes his heart race.
His wife is there with his young son,
His hero's welcome has now begun.
And all the while his heart beats fast,
The panic within him cannot last.
He hopes his fears will now start to wane,
'Cos all the while he's smiling; he's thinking he's insane.

His lover runs across the way,
His words are thoughts he cannot say.
She hugs him tight and holds his head to hers,
A car backfires, he jumps and swears.
His son doesn't know him and starts to cry,
He wishes he could just curl up and die.
His wife ignores his haunted look,
Cannot see that he is now a closed book.
He wants to feel happy now he's home,
No more in that futile land need he roam.
But every moment fills him with dread,
He wishes it was not his mate but him who was dead.

His sleep is fitful every night,
Every noise gives him a fright.
He cannot kiss his wife with ease,
Even though this does her displease.
The last person he held that tight,
Died in his arms that fateful night.
His heart it races all the time,
He cannot drive for fear of a landmine.
His mates they take him on the piss,
'Cos his laughter and jokes they do miss.
But one drink later he's had enough,
He doesn't really give a stuff.
He feels nothing for his wife, his son,
His hero's nightmare has begun.

He tells his doctor how he feels,
The doctor says time will heal.
He goes to visit his mate's grave,
Sees the words on it engraved:
Private Jones aged twenty-one
Killed by a roadside bomb.
He goes back home, gets things in order,
Doesn't know he's got post-traumatic stress disorder.

Takes an overdose of pills,
Slowly his pulse beats to a still.
His soldier days are over now,
The haunted frown has left his brow.

No hero's funeral for this boy,
His own life he took, did destroy.
An unspoken feeling left behind,
That no one helped him with his mind.
No injury or scars did they see,
No crutch or wheelchair needed he.
Yet day by day his heart bled dry,
And now for him they stand and cry.
Another statistic of a war,
But this boy's not a hero, not any more.

The Medal

~~~

AIRCRAFTSMAN JOHN GIFFARD (82)

Royal Air Force, National Service (United Kingdom) 1947–9

In the town of Wootton Bassett the streets are quiet again
As the watchers on the pavement stand silent in the rain.
While the sombre line of hearses with their coffins travel by
Although my heart is aching, I'm far too numb to cry.

And as they slowly pass me they all look just the same.
I don't know which of them is Joe. I could not see his name.
A lady close beside me began to say a prayer.
I wondered how a loving god could cause such great despair.

They said Joe was a hero. His actions saved his force.
I wish he hadn't done it, though I'm proud of him of course.
He always was impulsive and wouldn't stop to think.
To help his mates in trouble he'd be there in a wink.

I had to tell the children. They idolised their dad.
Young Michael couldn't understand. He's just a little lad.
I said, 'He's with the angels.' He said, 'You should be glad.
If he is in a better place why are you all so sad?'

Poor Mary's devastated, her world is torn apart.
I hear her sobbing in the night. It really breaks my heart.
But I must hide my feelings and cannot show my pain
Although I know I'll never feel his loving touch again.

My friends have rallied round us and tried to comfort me
But none of them can realise how empty life can be.
Unless you've lost a loved one, you really cannot know
Just what it's like and how I feel now I no more have Joe.

I'm summoned to the Palace. I'm going to meet the Queen.
I'm sure she will be very kind as others all have been.
        But what we're to be given can't compensate our loss,
A shiny piece of metal,
A Military Cross?

Shame

—∿—

SERGEANT JOHN 'BJ' LEWIS (37)
Royal Air Force, Iraq (Operation Telic) 2008

We proudly served and followed the flag,
hailed as heroes – liberators of Iraq.
We fought with courage, faced the ultimate test,
with honour and valour we all tried our best.

We achieved our objectives, forced the change of regime,
counted our dead, young lives wasted it seems:
As with hindsight we're told that our conduct was woeful,
journalists clamour to point it out as unlawful.

Headlines cry out with tales of abuse,
we're painted as killing for fun, no excuse.
An illegal invasion, a political game,
an embarrassing endeavour that now carries great shame.

So what now for the veterans who were sent for the cause?
Who were told it was just, and believed that it was.
Who trusted the government that said it was right,
who out of duty were obliged to enter the fight.

We endured much hardship to do the right thing,
with no concept of the guilt and great shame it would bring.
How could we have known when we first answered the call
that we'd be consigned to the history books as not right at all?

The Repatriation

—◇—

PRIVATE NATHAN GUNAPALAN (23)

The London Regiment, Afghanistan (Operation Herrick) 2010

As I stood there rooted to the spot
one amongst hundreds I am all alone,

the wail of the bagpipes,
the look from the corner of my eye,
is this real, it can't be, but there they were,
their caskets draped in the red, white and blue of the Union Jack,
Their soulless bodies being carried on the shoulders of
    tearful friends.

As they pass, a brace* from a sergeant major, a salute from a
    commanding officer
and the sad bewildered stares from a hundred lost souls,
laid to rest aboard the aircraft, the rear doors slowly shut,
as if a coffin itself,
a sense of finality, a sense of sorrow and loss.
Still standing we looked on as the grey bird in the sky dipped
    its wing in tribute
then took them home.

---

* *Stand up straight and to attention (in uniform) comes from 'brace*
ourselves'

Confusion

Dedicated to Privates Robbie Laws,
Gavin Elliott and their families

———

MAJOR STEWART HILL (40)

Royal Welsh, Afghanistan (Operation Herrick) 2009

My last memory in Afghanistan
Watching with sadness
The helicopter that took my dead and injured soldiers away
The first tragedy for my company
How should I tell them?

These thoughts were interrupted
replaced by shrapnel in my brain from another explosion
How little I knew
No awareness of the knock on my wife's door
My worried colleagues nor the shards that tore through my skull

Thankfully I have no memory
Of the pain my family suffered
Nor my own affliction
For that you will have to ask my bedside companions

I am told that upon waking
I tried to escape
I was trapped and captured by the Taliban
Days of explanation reduced my fear
But bewilderment remained

I became aware that something was wrong a few weeks later
A painful head and deafness accompanied by a constant shrill
Disorientation and weight loss
A few visitors but only slight comprehension
But how were my soldiers?
I missed them and prayed for their safety

Exhaustion, imbalance and dysfunctional thoughts
Delivered by an explosive device
Annoyed at the disruption to my work
Like my brain, ripped apart from those I loved
To the welcome fold of those I love much more
But in unfortunate circumstances

Over time the tangible confusion has subsided to a lesser one
With how my brain now functions
Deafness and tinnitus remain an integral part of my life
Nearly two years later and this journey continues
A most frustrating and emotional one
For my family as well

Life with a Brain Injury

——~~——

MAJOR STEWART HILL (40)

Royal Welsh, Afghanistan (Operation Herrick) 2009

Our brains make us who we are
Mine is now different
A complex organ degraded by injury

Most days I feel inefficient
A Land Rover engine, insufficient
For an armoured vehicle

Reduced capacity to drive
With the power and speed
I used to, I want to, I feel, I need

Enforced change in cognition, behaviour, personality
I have changed but how to explain the difficulty
Obvious to me but not you?

Thirty-nine years of personal development stubbed out,
Like the post-firefight cigarettes we smoked about
In Afghanistan

No longer can I serve to lead,
Although I plead,
Just to see again, the person I grew to be

Imagine
Waking up a different person
Altered for the rest of your life

How do you deal with it?
With sadness, strife,
Medication

My life has changed irrevocably
A challenge so unexpected
One that I am not sure I can win
Though one I have to face

A Child's Memory of War

—∿—

OLIVIA HILL (11)

Daughter of Major Stewart Hill, Afghanistan (Operation Herrick) 2009

As the days pass on,
I remember the day,
That brought us all together again,
From the separation of Afghanistan.

Looking at the bed that holds my daddy
Sleeping in a mind of unconsciousness,
Dreaming of space and eternity.
I remember the way he slept,
I remember the way he lay.

I see my daddy wake,
Feeling puzzled and confused,
I see my daddy crying,
Hurt in his eyes,
I know what he is thinking,
His family and friends
And the unfortunate ones who have now died.

God bless all of the soldiers,
Pray for them,
If only the Taliban could see what they were destroying,
The brave and loved ones who are now
Just memories.

I see my daddy get up,
From where he lay on his bed,
Scars and scabs around him.
Holding onto the walls
Helping him balance
Walking across the gleaming floor.

I remember the tubes all up his arms,
The bandages and plasters.
Him not being able to manage walking,
Then being put in a wheelchair,
Wheeling across the floor
Determined, once again, to take his first steps.

Soldier

~~~

CORPORAL CAMERON JOWETT (26)

The Mercian Regiment (Worcesters and Foresters),

Afghanistan (Operation Herrick) 2009

I have been where many won't go, where death is all around,
Where bullets fly and people die, bombs buried underground,
I'm different from your average man, I fight for what is right,
'Stand Firm', 'Strike Hard' is what I do with all my Mercian
    might.
I do not fight for Queen and country; I fight for all my friends,
Because they're the ones who'll have your back, from the start
    to the bitter end,
They're the ones who'll carry you if you should go 'man down'!
They're the ones who'll fight all day, for each other, not the
    Crown.

I have been where many won't; I've seen a lot of hurt,
I've been in fights with Taliban, rounds passing through my shirt,
I've run towards the enemy not knowing if I'll die,
You'd understand the pains of war if you'd seen a grown
    man cry;
Not crying because of fear! But crying for loss and regret,
We think and say every day, 'We shall never forget',
We've got to keep on fighting, despite the sudden pain,
We've got to 'Stand Firm, Strike Hard', or our friends have
    died in vain.

War is not a pretty thing, nor is it a silly game,
War is rotten and savage; war is full of pain,
War is cruel and scary, war is very strange,
War is a lot more dangerous than walking down a range.
So leave it to the soldier, who guards you day and night,
Over in Afghanistan, where he continues the bloody fight,
The soldier will not talk to you about what he has seen,
Just take his very word on it: he's been! he's seen!

Courageous Restraint on R&R

—∿—

MAJOR BARRY ALEXANDER (40)

Queen Alexandra's Royal Army Nursing Corps (QARANC) Nursing Officer,

Afghanistan (Operation Herrick) 2007

Long days in the pub
Mates at work
Drinking too much again
Time on my hands
Killing hands killing time

Beery bonhomie starts to grate
Turns into something else
A sneery comment, a nasty jibe
Fists fly furiously
Punches thrown first, followed by glasses

Rage descends
Head makes contact with nose
Right uppercut, a sickening crunch
Elbow to face, knee to groin
The fat civilian slides to the floor
Just desserts

Composure recovered; fix him with a steely glare
The fight a fleeting fantasy, what might have been
I think I had better leave
In the dark street the leaves whirl and scratch at the lamp posts
At home, in Helmand, courageous restraint is never easy

Coward

—◦◦◦—

CAPTAIN JAMES JEFFREY (32)

Queen's Royal Lancers, Afghanistan (Operation Herrick) 2009

I move among the people eyes down
Carrying no visible scars for proof
Merely returned, blending into mediocrity.
I know that I remained secure
Sealed within the operations room
Calling to those playing Russian roulette
On horrid, unforgiving Afghan ground.
I heard their destruction
Radios blaring anguished news,
Soldiers shouting, calling for back-up.
I imagined their terror then,
Now see their scars in altered bodies
The raw, crumpled,
Freakish folds of repaired skin.
I see the surgeon's work
The politician's choice
The people's lot.
I stand in the shower physically whole
Touching what they have lost
Yet cannot touch what I have lost
Not knowing exactly what it is or where it was.
I move among the people eyes down.

They Don't Seem to Realise

—◊◊◊—

CAPTAIN JAMES JEFFREY (32)

Queen's Royal Lancers, Afghanistan (Operation Herrick) 2009

Your family think you're being miserable
Getting annoyed with sullen moods
It's understandable, getting annoyed yourself
But it's hard to do much about it

For it comes stalking at any time
Relentless in its pressure
Squeezing out continual questions of
Imagined scenarios replayed, reconfigured

There's no point which is the bitch of it
But it all keeps looping round and round
Weaving into the mind's sinews and crevasses
Like gnarled rotted roots they spread out

Wrapping tentacles about seething nerves
Anaconda squeezing air out of your mind
Leaving it weak, dull, devoid, worn through
So that sometimes you just stare silently

Running on empty in your head
Which others assume is a sulk
Perhaps it is
Although it is indeed hard to say much

Thinking of dead children
The bags of scooped-up flesh
Which you don't have to see to comprehend
Oh no, the secret is

The knowing misery can still get out and find you
War's a vivid thing and likes a vivid imagination.

My Heart Beats Faster

—◦◦◦—

SERGEANT JOHN 'BJ' LEWIS (37)
Royal Air Force, Iraq (Operation Telic) 2008

A bee wakes me as it buzzes at my bedroom window,
it makes my heart beat faster.
An engine backfires in the shopping-centre car park,
it makes my heart beat faster.
A car door slams in the quiet of the night,
it makes my heart beat faster.
I find myself surrounded in a crowded shop,
it makes my heart beat faster.

You see for that split second, I've no control,
all are things that you would pay no heed.
But my subconscious takes over, just for that moment
and the instinct for survival makes my heart beat faster.

The bee sounds like a call to prayer from a distant minaret,
travelling on the still wind of the dusty desert plains
and my heart beats faster.

The backfire makes the boy racers laugh,
but all my mind hears is small arms fire
and my heart beats faster.

No one else even stirs as the door slams shut,
but I'm wrenched awake by the sound of incoming mortars
and my heart beats faster.

The shoppers jostle for the bargains,
high shelves are bursting with goods,
But I can see nowhere to hide, my escape route is blocked,
one well-placed bomb would kill us all . . .
My mind screams and my heart beats faster.

4

remembrance

Missing Person

—∿∿—

MICHAEL BRETT (55)
London Press Officer, Former Republic of Yugoslavia,
Bosnia-Herzegovina 1994–6

There are no roses at the end,
No raised glasses, no speeches,
As a missing person makes the world lighter,
Leaves everyone with a kind of debt.

A name that has no one floats away
Like a dropped holiday photograph
Of no one waving from lost blue seas.

A ghost's bedroom is guarded like a prince's,
By mothers, wives, and soldier ranks
Of empty suits and empty shoes.
A ghost has an answering machine but no home.

The parabolas of jets and bombs,
Lead to a new geological age, to fossil lives.
They leave no place, no centre, for love to go to;
Love can just catch trains of half-remembered conversations
That lead only to pictures of a ghost.

Firemen, soldiers, the enquiring spades that probe as shrapnel,
Police dogs. These are guests at a kind of wedding
Where ghost and man fuse.

Behind 'Police Line Don't Cross' tapes,
A policewoman with his wallet blots out the sun.

The Evening Standard, *27 January 2011*

'350 UK deaths in Afghanistan'

—◊◊◊—

COLONEL SIMON MARR, MBE (46)

Royal Regiment of Fusiliers,

Afghanistan (Operation Herrick) 2007 and 2010

Front page:

Police on rack in phone-hacking scandal.

Economy poll strikes low note.

Fears as Mandela goes into hospital.

Star backing for sexism row pair.

Teachers' power to search pupils.

Second page:

Smash-and-grab

Jewellery raiders await sentencing.

Para killed while helping comrade.

Scalextric powers up for Olympic bikes.

Public's hope of recovery falters, says new poll.

Employment law 'will let bosses hire and fire at will'.

Third page:

Won over – award for loved-up Cowell

'We'd have been sacked a hundred times'

– Clarkson steps into sexism row.

Reports of War

~~~

CORPORAL DANNY MARTIN (28)

1 Staffords Battle Group, Iraq (Operation Telic) 2003 and 2005

Before I grew old, I was made of stone
Granite; igneous, solid.
Before sand wore
down my chiselled jaw, dulled my steely eyes.
Salute this hero!
With twenty-one guns, salute!

In my home hear echoes of that salute
ricochet off walls of plaster, and deeper, stone.
While souls of heroes
freeze to a solid
mass. Their eyes
iced shut by war.

My pen only moves to write of war.
Its marks will spell a scrawled salute
(yes, yet again), and I'll
talk about names carved in stone
again. It's solid
to avoid repetition when the end of heroes

is here. What now for these who thrive on heroes?
Who gorge themselves on fruits of war?
Who found an excuse, and so led
the armies, took the salute?

Purses of power freefall to stone
broke. Tabloid outrage sparks in their eyes.

Can you see your heart in their eyes?
A heart aching for heroes;
a heart of ice, a heart of stone?
When you get your own kicks from war
(like the goosebump prickles you feel when Hollywood heroes
    salute)
You make the future of war more solid.

Future of my skin, future of my solid
core. I'll
twitch in my sleep – nocturnal salutes
to that drawing-down of blinds. Blinds that rose
again in the morning. War
repeated. Like names carved in stone.

If you get solid at the thought of heroes.
If you feel wet pricks in your eyes at the thought of war.
Salute the man. Salute the stone.

The Old Soldier's View

PRIVATE KEN PICKLES (72)

Gordon Highlanders, Cold War

It seems to some who served their country;
Those lucky enough to return safely home
To a land, they said, 'Fit for Heroes'
But from our history books reminding us of Rome
And the fall of an empire once mighty
Like ours so recently has been
Where compared to our political masters
A soldier's life is honourable and clean!

But it's selfless you see, that's the difference
And how would they know about that?
For bravery, courage and honour
Are virtues they seemingly lack!
It's their boasting, their falsehoods, and their spindrift
Which is like froth on a pint of the best;
So 'cheers' to my brothers and comrades,
The Good Lord will deal with the rest!

Anonymous

—∿∿—

PRIVATE ERIC COTTAM (91)
Royal Warwickshire Regiment, Second World War (Dunkirk) 1940

We, in this home, are old, very old.
We roll back the years by comradely remembering
as we wait for God's judgement.

I was 'awarded' two medals.
That is why I was allowed here
when the nurse who devotedly wifed me all those years
died.

Just two bland medals,
one for each missing limb, I wryly joke.

The two ubiquitous medals,
now smiling brightly at me,
lie on their pristine unattached ribbons.
Unworn.

They lie alone,
waiting for an absent companion campaign medal.
And time is running out.

'Campaign medals are awarded only for victories, old chap,
and Dunkirk was a defeat, after all.'

If this was Churchill's view,
did he remember Gallipoli?

Fish
The River Murrell under Wireless Ridge, February 2007

————

CAPTAIN ROGER FIELD (55)

Blues and Royals, Falklands War (Falkland Islands) 1982

Peace: a sea trout on a river which once knew death.

Understanding: a hook that sweeps the river to snare a fish,
where bullets once churned the water to snare a life.

Victory: a fish for supper,
not a body for the pit.

That is healing,
twenty-five years later.

Pity, perhaps, the fish.

Looking Forward

—◊◊◊—

SERGEANT JOHN 'BJ' LEWIS (37)
Royal Air Force, Iraq (Operation Telic) 2008

Keen to survive the last attack,
don't want my name etched on a plaque:
'in memory of those who fell in Iraq'
I don't want a coffin to carry me back.

Go home to all those that I hold dear.
Relax, and enjoy having nothing to fear.
Forget all the hardship and hold loved ones near;
look forwards, not back, with a conscience that's clear.

Take pride in the knowledge that I did my best,
wear a shiny new medal upon my chest.
Restart my life with new vigour and zest,
thank the good fortune that kept me blessed.

But for those still out here I'll not forget,
that it's you here, not I, I owe you a debt,
I know what you'll go through, the challenges set,
I wish you good luck with my utmost respect.

Remembering

~~~

CORPORAL CAMERON JOWETT (26)

The Mercian Regiment (Worcesters and Foresters),

Afghanistan (Operation Herrick) 2009

When I'm alone I stare into space and think about my mates,
who lost their lives far from home and went to St Peter's Gate.
When I think about these times, I hang my head and cry,
I always ask myself the question: 'Why them, God, why?'
It's sad to think two years ago 'Sandy' went away,
he lost his life in a town the Afghans named Rahim Kalay.
I'll never forget that bloody day, the date was June the 6th,
When rockets flew and fears grew that bad it made you sick.

It's sad to think two years ago 'Wrighty' lost the fight,
he was a man full of humour, to know him was a delight,
he made me smile all the time, he was my bestest friend,
I'll never forgive the people who brought his life to an end.
I'll always remember 'Wrighty'; I'll never forget his smile,
He tried hard whatever he did; he'd always go the extra mile,
but it's bye for now young comrade, until I meet my 'fate',
just promise me one thing Tom, you'll meet me at the gate.

It's sad to think this very year 'Hilly' lost his life,
'Stand Firm', 'Strike Hard' is what he did, he made the sacrifice.
I'll never forget this brave young man, he gave all that he had,
Fighting against the Taliban in a place called 'Hassanabad'.
I know if he was here today, he wouldn't change at all,
he'd still be a professional soldier, who stood at 'six foot four',

he'd still be out there on the ground with all his Mercian
    brothers,
fighting side by side again! And looking after one another.

But even though I stare into space and remember their
    tragic ends,
I try my best to think about why they were such good friends,
I think about what I would say if we could meet again,
But I won't tell you what I'd say, it's 'between me and them'.

We will remember them.

Wootton Bassett (after Thomas Hardy)

—〰—

MICHAEL BRETT (55)

London Press Officer, Former Republic of Yugoslavia,

Bosnia-Herzegovina 1994–6

They buried Gunner Frost beside the church
Where all the Frosts had always lain
In their high-tide marks of quiet lives,
But Gunner Frost was not the same:

Where giant skies meet giant hills
Gunner Frost was quietly killed.

Yet part of that far land
Will Gunner Frost forever be,
While Afghan mud is still on his hands,
While Afghan girls still go to school.

His life melted in the Afghan spring
And down Death's rivers floated home
On the shoulders of enormous men
And in the cargo holds of planes;

And those who saw his coffin pass
Counted it their private loss

And stood in silence like the snow.

And in Other News

WARRANT OFFICER MICHAEL SAUNDERS (37)
The Mercian Regiment (Worcesters and Foresters),
Afghanistan (Operation Herrick) 2009

On the news you will hear it said,
'In Helmand, another soldier's dead.'
But quickly on the news will go,
So quickly that you may never know,
Know the soldier's hopes and fears,
The sacrifice of stolen years.
Of friends and family with no relief,
From a prison built with bars of grief.
Know the regret of things left unsaid,
And the sorrow of things said instead.
Of plans and hopes unfulfilled,
With the fallen soldier killed.
So think in future if you can,
Behind the headline stands the man.

My Father Walking

~~~

Mrs Liz Davies (64)

Daughter of Gunner Wilfred Gibbens,

Second World War (Tobruk, now Libya) 1941

I remember my father walking, walking,
Walking sandy bushveldt paths for miles,
Feet shifting in his soft, worn boots,
Brown arms swinging from wide shoulders,
Long legs moving his body along.
He learned this walk as a farm boy,
Walking tireless and on for miles
Searching thickets and rocks for wayward beasts
In his loose loping kind of style. In old photos
He looks from under his helmet with deep-set eyes;
They came in handy, those fifty-mile stares,
As he scanned horizons the war years away
In the desert sun, while the twenty-five pounders
Roared, spat fire, and shook him to the bone,
Until History overtook him and roped him
Into years in a prison camp, wasted years
Of hard forced labour, and cruel cold.
He told us, little brother and me, of his war
In a jovial voice that made light of it all,
Like an action movie with sound effects,
But it was in dead earnest. He came home
With legs pitted by shrapnel, showed us the scars
Down hollowed calves; lungs fretted with cold, he said,
Skin stretched pale over ribs, teeth loose and bad,

Hearing gone and face sunk in. And safe at home
He slept a while, ate softly, remembered slow,
Till one day he woke strong, got up and walked again.

Humility

—◊—

COLONEL HUGO FLETCHER (55)

16 Air Assault Brigade, Northern Ireland 1981, 82, 88–89, 92 and 95

Peacock proud,
A mile high,
Shoulders back,
Head in sky,
I felt good
Walking by.

Combat-tried
subaltern,
Different from
other men,
So I thought
Smugly then.

Saw MacDonald
In the town,
Ancient, wizened,
Tumbledown,
Somebody
I'd always known.

Owned the local
Tailor's store,
'Established
Eighteen ninety-four'
Considered him
A crashing bore.

Swaggered past,
Caught his eye
Recognised
My Airborne tie,
Face lit up
'My, oh my!'

'Hello sir,
Good to see
You a Para,
Just like me!'
Him a Para?
Can this be?

'Sicily
In forty-three,
Wounded in
Back and knee,
Nearly was
Death of me.'

'Forty-five
Crossed the Rhine
Lives were lost,
But not mine,
Tailor's shop
suited fine.'

Unsung hero,
Old and grey
Doesn't look
Much today,
Did it all
Yesterday.

All's not as
It seems to be
Meeting him
Taught to me
A lesson in
Humility.

Village War Memorial

—∽∽—

ABLE SEAMAN RALPH WOOLNOUGH (86)
Royal Navy, Second World War 1944

Including land
You cost seven hundred quid,
Which doesn't sound much now.
A fortune in the twenties though.
All by subscription, too.
A penny here, a tanner there . . .

Last year some bastards pinched the paving stones.

But we're still here.
Though not as many wearing medals:
More councillors, and people of that sort.

I kept my medals in a drawer
For fifty years. Then put them on
Self-consciously.
A chap said, 'Are they summat special, like?
Or were they just for being there?'
'No,' I said. 'Not special.
I got them just for being there.'

A cold spot this, in November.
I'll get around the back, as usual,
Before the parish clerk reads out the names.
    Just names.

No one knows them now
Although they are set in stone.

This year they have dug up a bugler from somewhere.
I hope he doesn't drag it out,
With the rainclouds coming in
And black already over Pendle.

Two minutes won't mean much to you
You've stood here all the year in silence.

I stand, head bowed,
And think of nothing much.
I've read about these chaps
Who still feel guilty they survived.
    I'm not.
    I'm glad.
    Bloody glad I've had another sixty years.
    Otherwise, what would have been the point?

Perhaps there never was much point.
Perhaps you're just a monument to waste.

To The Fallen.

You should have fallen too,
On that bastard late at night
Who dug up all the paving stones.

Multi-Coloured Goodbye

—∿∿—

MAJOR SUZY AYERS (53)
Queen Alexandra's Royal Army Nursing Corps (QARANC) Head of
Department for Theatres, Afghanistan (Operation Herrick) 2006 and 2010

We came as one in the fading sun,
caps, grey, green, blue, black, maroon.
To say goodbye to a special man,
a pioneer, a searcher.
It was death he found as he cleared the ground
– for others

We heard of him from his friends
'The first in line'
'Brave'
'A friend to all'
'No one can fill the hole
– of chatterbox'

We cannot say why
it was his time to die.
To honour the life he gave,
we came to salute him
on his way home.
'Rest in Peace Charlie'

Shot Through
1919–95

—◆—

JAMIE WARDE-ALDAM (54)
Son of Major Julian Warde-Aldam, Second World War 1939–45

I visited Geoffrey
one summer. He was
a short bus ride out of
town in a graveyard.

I hadn't prepared to see
the family name
in stone under the white
Sicilian sun.
Young. You don't think.

And I don't think Daddy
was ready, when some-
one sidled up to him
in a German camp
and said, 'I was with your
brother when he died.
If you want to know what
happened, I'm around.'

What had happened was this:
he'd been sawn half through
by machine-gun bullets
somewhere near the beach
close to Siracusa.

In the field hospital,
he'd lived for a week.
Stretchered, injected, dressed,
sutured and trollied
through a limbo of
morphine, chaos and pain.

When Daddy came back, he
could no more say what
had happened than shout fuck
in a church service.

He didn't know if his
family knew what
he knew. Until his ma,
years later, let slip
with 'At least we know Geoff
was killed instantly.'

When he started to fail
(they're his words, not mine)
the horrors he'd kept to
himself through kindness
returned to beat him.

And I believe they did.
Defeated him, flat.
Wars (he knew anyway)
don't respect ceasefires,
they like to keep going.

The Last Supper

—◊◊◊—

CAPTAIN JAMES JEFFREY (32)

Queen's Royal Lancers, Afghanistan (Operation Herrick) 2009

A supper when we shared a table
Secure beside the bomb-blast walls
The ketchup bottle a reminder of home
Stands out from many others

I remember your humour, the polite bearing
Explaining that insane job with zeal
Each day spending hours defusing bombs
Lying on dirt tracks, staring through sweat at wires

I sat wondering how it must feel
Almost asking the unquestionable
Might it be a matter of time with the numbers?
Perhaps you'd already thought this through

Yet you never deterred in protecting others
All the way to where you could not turn back
From the blinding hot blast demanding sacrifice
Taking away the scruffy cheerful calm

Leaving another picture in a morose mosaic.